SOMALIA
IN WORD
AND IMAGE

Edited by
Katheryne S. Loughran
John L. Loughran
John William Johnson
Said Sheikh Samatar

Published by the Foundation for Cross Cultural Understanding, Washington, D.C.,
in cooperation with Indiana University Press, Bloomington

Manufactured in the United States of America

Library of Congress Cataloging-in-Publication Data

Main entry under title:

Somalia in word and image.

    Catalog of an exhibition.
    Bibliography: p.
    1. Somalia — Social life and customs — Exhibitions.
2. Ethnology — Somalia — Exhibitions. 3. Material culture —
Somalia — Exhibitions. I. Loughran, Katheryne S.
II. Foundation for Cross Cultural Understanding.
DT402.2.S66   1986   967'.73'00740153   85-45470
ISBN 0-253-35360-2 (Indiana University Press)
ISBN 0-253-20376-7 (Indiana University Press : pbk.)

1 2 3 4 5 90 89 88 87 86

CONTENTS

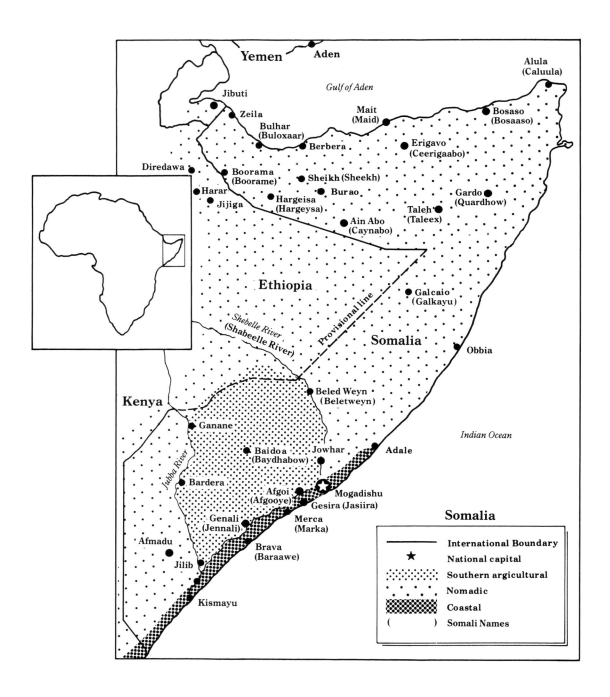

Yemen   Aden

Gulf of Aden   Alula
                                               (Caluula)

Jibuti   Mait   Bosaso
      Zeila   (Maid)   (Bosaaso)
   Bulhar
   (Buloxaar)   Erigavo
         Berbera   (Ceerigaabo)

Diredawa
        Boorama   Sheikh (Sheekh)
        (Boorame)
  Harar   Burao   Gardo
     Jijiga Hargeisa   (Quardhow)
             (Hargeysa)   Taleh
                   Ain Abo   (Taleex)
                   (Caynabo)

              Ethiopia   Galcaio
                                          (Galkayu)

        Shebelle River
        (Shabeelle River)   Somalia   Obbia

Kenya   Beled Weyn
                              (Beletweyn)

        Ganane   Indian Ocean

                   Baidoa   Jowhar   Adale
                   (Baydhabow)
      Bardera
              Afgoi   Mogadishu
              (Afgooye) Gesira (Jasiira)
        Genali   Merca   Somalia
        (Jennali)   (Marka)
  Afmadu
     Jilib   Brava
                (Baraawe)

         Kismayu

	International Boundary
★	National capital
	Southern argicultural
	Nomadic
	Coastal
( )	Somali Names

FOREWORD

In *Voyage of A Naturalist,* Charles Darwin tells of the furor he created among the so-called educated elite of a certain South American country when he told them that the earth was a sphere. Until then, they had believed otherwise, although the bit of scientific information he was passing along was 2,000 years old at the time. For many of us, the revelations brought by this catalogue and the exhibition it introduces will be of the same character — a quiet furor, perhaps, but a furor nonetheless — demolishing old stereotypes and creating fresh images through which we may begin to understand the physical and imaginative world of the Somali peoples living their lives on a remote littoral of the Horn of Africa, far removed from the air and ship corridors of international travel.

The Somali coast has always exerted a certain fascination for the Western voyager, who saw the land and its people only in fragments, always in mystery, never in wholeness. For the Portuguese circumnavigators of the fifteenth century, it was a barren headland en route to India, visited the first time with disastrous consequences. For Richard Burton in the nineteenth century, it was a hostile passage he crossed en route to Harar. The photographs of orbiting Apollo missions have revealed to us with incredible clarity the Horn of Africa's physical shape and contours — a harsh red wasteland glimpsed through patterns of cumulus astride the Indian Ocean — but the mystery remains, even more seductive than before.

The triumph of this book and the exhibit that accompanies it is that it can be a mystery no longer. Even for those of us who have lived in Somalia and who grew to love the land and its people, it is a book of continuing revelation, a book of such astonishing images, of light, color, vistas, and surfaces, that even the least intrepid among us will know that he too has traveled there. Imagination can do no more.

Samuel Hamrick

GRANTORS

This exhibition and catalogue have been most generously supported by grants from the Ministry of Culture and Higher Education of the Somali Democratic Republic and The National Endowment for the Humanities.

LENDERS TO THE EXHIBITION

Asha Addou, Mogadishu
Lee Cassanelli, Philadelphia, Pennsylvania
Giovanni Ferrero, Rome
Maria Ferrero, Milano
Foundation for Cross Cultural Understanding, Washington, D.C.
Martin and Evelyn Ganzglass, Washington, D.C.
John and Elizabeth Johnson, Bloomington, Indiana
Peter and Karin Koch, The Hague
Virginia Luling, London
Museum of Natural History, New York City
National Museum of African Art, Smithsonian Institution, Washington, D.C.
Somali National Museum, Mogadishu
Abby Thomas, Washington, D.C.

ACKNOWLEDGEMENTS

As the first major project of the Foundation for Cross Cultural Understanding "Somalia in Word and Image" is also the first major exhibition and catalogue to deal with this material. The culmination of four years of work by countless people here and abroad, it owes its genesis to a group of scholars whose immediate, enthusiastic gift of time and wisdom continued to help guide the project toward becoming a reality. It is more than appropriate, therefore, that our first acknowledgement should be to them: To John W. Johnson, Indiana University, B.W. Andrzejewski and Ioan Lewis, University of London, Said Sheikh Samatar, Rutgers University, Virginia Luling, University of London, Lee Cassanelli, University of Pennsylvania, Linda Donley, University of Cambridge and Ebrahim Noor Sherif, Rutgers University. For their participation our gratitude is immeasurable.

At Indiana University a group of people gave us support without which the preparation of this exhibition and catalogue could never have been accomplished. Already involved in a multitude of other responsibilities, Roy Sieber, Professor of Fine Arts, never hesitated to provide encouragement and careful guidance in matters of concept and content. His help was frequently facilitated by Sophia Sieber who played an important role in our communications system. From the associates of the African Studies Program, beginning with its Director, Patrick O'Meara, we received unfailing personal friendship and individual insights which touched every aspect of the project. Our thanks must go to Brian Winchester and Mary Jo Arnoldi whose participation was myriad. The generous editorial advice of Ivan Karp; the skill with which David Binkley guided us to our exhibition deadline; the cheerful spirits of Judith Wilkinson and Sue Hanson in times of crises: these are memories which are a privilege to acknowledge.

The educational components were conceived with great imagination by B.W. Andrzejewski and independent radio producer Robert Montiegel. From the field trip in Somalia and long hours in the studio, assisted by the constant professionalism of sound engineer James Anderson, their conception was realized in two radio documentaries and an audio-visual presentation. As a member of the field team Phoebe Ferguson brought meticulous selection of effective material to the photographic record which she achieved. In Somalia, research and logistical assistance were provided by the members of the Somali National Academy of Arts and Sciences, the Somali National Museum, Radio Mogadishu and Radio Hargeisa. Warm hospitality was accorded us throughout the nation. Our deep gratitude must go to Anita and Suleiman Adan for their immediate endorsement of the project. Anita Suleiman, along with Lisbeth Loughran, was also responsible for field coordination in Somalia and their contribution to the outreach materials was essential to our success. Crisanne Albers and Edward Mazuroski never failed to help us cope with shipment of the objects for the exhibition. Faduma Jama Gibril, Kristyne Loughran, Sheila Andrzejewski, Karen Koch, Jay Kernis, Asha Addou, Martha MacInnis, Abby Thomas and Daniel Walsh all offered hours of research, translation, cataloguing and editing. To Daniel Walsh we also owe the first working layout of the catalogue. Giovanni Ferrero gave generously of his time and enthusiasm throughout the project both here and in

Rome. Barbara Shortley managed to accommodate every travel plan at a moment's notice. For each of these people and their special talents our appreciation, in recollection, can only increase.

The pilot exhibition was organized and mounted by Larry O'Reilly, Betty Jo Kaveney and Ann Rosselli. At the University of Virginia, discriminating counsel came from David Lawall, Curator of the Bayly Museum, and in New York from Marie Therese Brincard, Director of the Art Exhibition Program at the African American Institute. Giorgio Giacomelli and Francesco Aluisi greatly facilitated our research in Rome where museum assistance was unstintingly provided by Valeria Petrucci and Alessandra Cardelli Antinori of the Museo L. Pigorini, by the members of the Istituto Italo-Africano and in London by the staff at the British Museum. Acknowledgement must be made to the museums which have loaned objects for this exhibition: The Somali National Museum, Mogadishu, the National Museum of African Art, Washington, D.C., and the Museum of Natural History, New York. "Somalia in Word and Image" would have been inconceivable without the generosity of the lenders to the exhibition. To them we owe so much, not only for their willingness to share these precious pieces but to provide the accompanying documentation. The successful initial installation of the exhibition at the Mathers Museum in Bloomington, Indiana was carried out by Jeff Conrad, David Schalliol, and Dot Anderson. The special skills of Judy Sylvester, Conservator, Mathers Museum, Bloomington, Indiana, and Rene Welfeld, Conservator, National Museum of African Art, Washington, D.C., were crucial in the handling of the most fragile among these pieces. Elizabeth Johnson, Lilly Rare Books Library, Bloomington, Indiana, staff at the James Ford Bell Library, University of Minnesota, Minneapolis, and at the Library of Congress, Washington, D.C., helped us in the often perplexing search for elusive old prints.

The encouragement of Sylvia Williams, Director of the National Museum of African Art, was essential in the publication of the catalogue. Constant too, in their support were Harold Campbell and Kay Cole in the preparation of the catalogue. Pauline DiBlasi's busy schedule never prevented her from consulting on the catalogue's design. Delmar Lipp's help was invaluable during the photographing of the objects from the earliest stages of the project. The generous contribution of Manfred Wehrmann's Somali photographs has greatly enhanced our image of Somalia and its people. The care taken with their reproduction must be credited to the members of the Washington House of Photography who worked with us on the exhibition and catalogue. The guidance of editors Johnson, Samatar and Arnoldi, as well as Janet Rabinowitch of Indiana University Press—witty, insightful, often exacting—made every step of the way to publication a fully shared and rewarding creative experience.

Extraordinary thanks are given to Abdullahi Omaar in London, whose magnanimous contribution helped to make our field trip a reality. Finally, the Foundation is indebted to the Ministry of Higher Education and Culture of the Somali Democratic Republic for the confidence and material support it has given us. Major funding for the exhibition and catalogue from the National Endowment for the Humanities is gratefully acknowledged. The encouragement and wise counsel of Anna Caravelli and Abby Cutter of the Endowment's Museum Program were instrumental in the successful completion of these projects.

John Louis Loughran
President, Foundation for Cross Cultural Understanding

DEDICATION

This book is for the late Musa Galaal. Revered as a student, historian, scholar and sage by all Somalis, he was with us from the beginning of our project. He enriched and deepened our work as he had enriched, deepened and given direction to the Somali peoples' appreciation of their poetic heritage and culture. In acknowledgement of our profound debt to Musa we dedicate this book to him, to his life's purpose and the Somali people he so loved.

THE CATALOGUE

THE MARKET PLACE in Mogadishu in 1882. From E. Cerulli, *Somalia, Scritti Vari Editi ed Inediti,* Vol. I., Fig. XIV. Istituto Poligrafico dello Stato, P.V., Rome 1957. Figure is referenced as *Dal Voyage chez les Benadirs* di G. Revoil. Figure courtesy Library of Congress.

INTRODUCTION
WORD AND IMAGE IN THE
HORN OF AFRICA

John William Johnson

S*omalia in Word and Image* represents the first major exhibition of Somali material art and artifacts in the United States. It is the result of several years of dedicated effort and planning by several organizations and many people, principally the Foundation for Cross Cultural Understanding, the Ministry of Culture and Higher Education of the Somali Democratic Republic, the African Studies Program at Indiana University, and numerous private individuals who gave of their time and expertise. Major funding for the exhibit has been provided by the Ministry of Culture and Higher Education, the National Endowment for the Humanities, the Foundation for Cross Cultural Understanding, and several private sources. The National Endowment for the Humanities also provided a second grant for the production of this catalogue. To all these agencies and people go the gratitude of the planners and organizers of *Somalia in Word and Image.*

Throughout the forty or more years that foreigners have conducted serious and extensive research on the Horn of Africa, it was consistently believed that Somalia was rich in oral traditions but poor in material culture. This contention was based on the assumed logic that because of the difficulty of transportation in a nomadic society, Somalis concentrated their creative efforts in oral art rather than material culture. In fact, no one bothered to conduct fieldwork on this subject because of this overriding assumption. While it is true that the nomadic majority of the land must keep possessions to a minimum because of the demands of the herding economy, it is also true that the coastal and agricultural sections of the country have no such limitations. Indeed, what has become obvious is that all Somalis, regardless of their economic orientation, have material folklore which is not only useful but also symbolically related to their world view and the context of their environment. A personal experience in Somalia will illustrate this point.

On my wedding day in Somalia, a friend came early to my house and presented me with a *hangool*, the nomadic tool for constructing corrals for livestock, forked on one end for uprooting thorn bushes and hooked on the other end for dragging them into place (see page 62). "You cannot become a *reer* [household, lineage, clan] without a *hangool*," my friend explained. The *hangool*, he said, was a traditional wedding gift for a man in Somalia. This ostensibly simple and functional tool, then, is also employed as a phallic symbol for manhood, representing the aspiration of every Somali man to be named the mythical head of a lineage segment in the distant future, generations after his death. The assumed paucity of material art in Somalia is a false impression that *Somalia in Word and Image* seeks to eliminate.

While field research for the art exhibit clearly demonstrates that Somalia, like all societies of the world, possesses material art and artifacts, it is also true that the spoken word, the oral folklore of Somalia, enjoys an overarching predominance vis-à-vis other modes of artistic expression in the country. During the planning stages of the exhibit, each time the cultural traditions of Somalia were considered, the oral tradition crept into the discussion. This fact reflected the reality of the predominance of oral art on the Horn of Africa, and there seemed no way to exhibit Somali material culture without somehow taking into account the importance of the spoken word and the relationship of material folklore to that of the verbal. Thus, *Somalia in Word and Image* also seeks to relate these two modes of artistic expression.

The purpose of this catalogue is twofold. First and obviously, it documents the artifacts shown in the exhibit. Choice objects from the show are represented here, as well as some that were not exhibited at every site because of limited exhibit space. While this catalogue cannot be definitive — neither was the show, for that matter — it goes a long way toward giving the reader the flavor of material arts and crafts in this part of eastern Africa.

The second purpose of this catalogue is to give the reader a flavor of the various environments in which these artifacts play a role. The essays treat various subjects relevant to Somali art, both oral and material. Again, our coverage is necessarily selective, and the interested reader may wish to seek out other writings for a fuller picture of this part of the world.

Conveying the atmosphere of Somalia is not easy in such a limited space. Somalia is a large and culturally diverse country. The territory of the Somali Democratic Republic, not including the Somali territories inside Kenya, Ethiopia, and Djibouti, is about the size of Texas. Although the Somalis represent a single ethnic block as far as social identity is concerned, there is considerable cultural diversity within this unity, and it was our concern that the exhibit reflect both this diversity and the cultural unity of the various regions of the country. Thus, the exhibit was divided into four sections. Three sections reflected the cultural diversity of Somalia by exhibiting art and artifacts from each of the three main economic orientations of the country: the nomadic herding, the interriverine agricultural, and the coastal mercantile areas. A fourth section reflected the cultural unity of Somalia through its religion, Islam. A brief description of these four represented segments of Somali culture will help introduce the reader to Somali society.

Most Somalis are herders of camels, cattle, sheep, and goats. They occupy all of the eastern Horn except the coast and the area between the Shabeelle and Jubba rivers. The economic orientation of the nomad is livestock: camels, sheep, goats, and in some places cattle and horses.

Seasonal migration separates the men from the women and children, as the men take the camels deep into the bush, where rainfall is not as crucial to the well-being of the camels as it is to that of the other livestock. Women and children herd the sheep and goats, which must remain closer to watering stations. Somali art and artifacts reflect this environmental context. Houses are portable and carried on the backs of burden camels from one site to another; mats of reed and skins are used in their construction. Milk vessels and other sorts of containers are made from materials found in the immediate environment. Trade and relations with kin who live in the other regions of Somalia and even abroad also enrich the material possessions of the nomads.

Between the two main rivers in Somalia, the Shabeelle and the Jubba, live those Somalis who practice agriculture, sometimes in combination with livestock rearing. Here a different group of Somali dialects is spoken, and a social organization different from that of the nomads can be found. Relying more on territorial alliance than on genealogical affiliation, these Somalis practice a form of agriculture which begins by firing the land to clear it. Traditionally, animals were not used in all of Somalia for plowing, but today the tractor is not an uncommon sight in this area. Since frequent travel is not the problem it is for the nomads, housing is more permanent. Round mud and wattle houses are constructed, often containing intricately carved doors and center post supports. Again, possessions are often constructed from environmentally available materials and are augmented by trade and connections with family in other regions of Somalia, principally in the cities.

Along the coast from just north of Muqdisho and continuing to the south can be found an old and complex mercantile culture. These cities, principally Muqdisho, Marka, and Baraawe, have rich traditions of *dhow* trade with Arabia, India, and even the Far East. Today, these cities also include communities of Somalis from all regions of the country, plus old communities of Arab and Persian immigrants. Some of their traditions, such as the *istun* stick fights at Afgooye, are shared with other non-contiguous groups throughout East Africa. Evidence exists that the new year celebrated by these groups of Somalis is the same as that in ancient Persia, suggesting migration older than any written sources can confirm. More than any other region of Somalia, this coastline has been the conduit of cultural exchange and borrowing. It often has been claimed that Somalis here have borrowed their cultural artifacts from their Swahili neighbors to the south, and even from more distant neighbors across the Indian ocean. While that can be demonstrated with many examples, some of these traditions, including material ones, may well have originated in the rich society of Shingaani and Xamar Weyn of old and been exported abroad from there. Again, records supporting the actual origins of many items found here simply do not exist. Moreover, items such as the carved wooden boxes (see page 117) resembling others along the Swahili coast were in fact carved in Somalia and have been incorporated into the traditions practiced on the Benaadir Coast, as this region is called.

Though regional differences in the actual practice of Islam exist in Somalia, religion nevertheless performs a major function of social and cultural unification. The great majority of Somalis are Moslems, whether they are able to worship in the thorn corral mosques characteristic of the countryside in the north, or in the magnificent architecture of the "Pakistani Mosque" in Muqdisho, characterized by its intricate mosaic tile. Prayer rugs and prayer beads, Koran holders, and clothing styles have all been influenced by Islam, but many of the actual artifacts used in the worship of God in Somalia were locally made and have become as much a part of Somali traditions as the *hangool* mentioned earlier. No exhibition concerning the Horn of Africa would be complete without extensive coverage of the practice of Islam.

The essays that follow also reflect the unity and diversity of the Somali people exhibited in *Somalia in Word and Image*.[1]

Mary Jo Arnoldi has written a broad overview of the material traditions in Somalia. Her essay carries readers through all the regions represented in the exhibit and orients them to the whole. Her discussion gives a historical perspective on the development of the material culture of Somalia.

Said Sheikh Samatar attempts in his essay to interconnect Somali verbal and visual arts chiefly in the nomadic sector. Said demonstrates the power that poetry commands in Somali social and political spheres, both as a force for the debate of political differences and as a means of pleading for peace and unity among its practitioners. He summarizes the use of objects of material culture as images in the poetry and the effect of this imagery on the rhetoric of verse.

The history of Somali literature, both oral and written, is the subject of the essay by B.W. Andrzejewski. He describes the oral nature of the poetry and explains some of the structures that enable Somalis to practice near verbatim memorization in their tradition. Andrzejewski further describes the impact of the tape recorder on the oral character of this poetry and its role in preserving these poems for future generations. He concludes by discussing the rise of Somali written literature and the role of the daily newspaper *Xiddigta Oktoobar* in this new development.

Some Somali scholars have claimed, perhaps with justification, that the nomadic north has received more than its fair share of attention from researchers into the traditions and history of Somalia. They sometimes refer to the problem as "Somali Prussianism." Lee V. Cassanelli's article goes a long way toward correcting this imbalance. The diversity of this area is placed into historical perspective, and the culture of the inter-riverine area is briefly described.

Through his description of the tradition of Somali wood engravings, Vinigi L. Grottanelli relates information about the Somali coast, thereby connecting this region to a larger tradition on the coast of Africa and in the even larger sphere of cultural influence which includes Arabia and India, and which has been nurtured for centuries by interaction and diffusion through migration and trade.

Finally, I.M. Lewis gives the reader an overview of the great social and cultural unity on the Horn of Africa by describing the particular Somali way of practicing Islam. His essay describes the historical role of the *wadaad*, or "holy man," in Somalia and the brotherhood movement there. He outlines the contributions of Somalis to the international cult of saints in Islam as a whole, and the role of religion in unifying Somalis against foreign intruders over the centuries.

For many years scholars of the Horn of Africa have claimed, and rightfully so, that the Somalis are fierce and independent, that they are very skilled indeed in the use of oral poetry and compose it for implementation in all aspects of their lives, including the political. They have, in fact, been called a nation of poets. While that is true, and work should continue on the all-important oral traditions, Somalis are also a nation of artists. The study of Somali art has been neglected, as has its customary and gestural folklore. *Somalia in Word and Image* represents a concerted effort to fill this gap in knowledge, and we hope it will be only a beginning in the study of these other traditions of Somalia, particularly the material. Much work remains to be done, and if we have inspired the progress of this work in some small way, then this exhibit and catalogue will have contributed positively to this aspiration.

GROUP OF SOMALIS. From *The Standard Library of Natural History, Embracing Living Animals and Living Races of Mankind,* Vol. V, Africa—Europe—America, p. 375. The University Society Inc., New York, 1911. The photograph is by Messrs. Negretti and Zambra, London.

THE ARTISTIC HERITAGE
OF SOMALIA

Mary Jo Arnoldi

Somalia, situated on the Horn of Africa, stands at the crossroads between Africa and the Near East and lies within a region of great cultural diversity. Today, the Somali people number about five million. Although the majority of Somalis live in the Somali Democratic Republic, substantial numbers can be found in the neighboring African countries of Djibouti, Ethiopia and Kenya.[1]

Somalis have a rich tradition of verbal and visual arts, which reflect both specific regional and shared forms and ideologies that are spread through the agency of Islam and long-standing trade networks. Since antiquity, Somalia has maintained commercial and cultural relationships with North Africa and the Arab peninsula. From 3100 to 350 B.C. Egypt imported frankincense and myrrh from the northeastern region of Somalia, the Biblical "Land of Punt."[2] Pre-Islamic Arabs and Persians founded trading entrepots at Zeila on the Gulf of Aden and Mogadishu on the east coast. In the seventh century, Islamicized Arabs strengthened these trading centers and introduced Islam to Somalia. Al Yaqubi, an Arab geographer writing in the ninth century, mentions both Zeila and Mogadishu as important commercial cities.[3] These centers exported ivory, hides, aromatic gums, slaves, spices, and cattle from the hinterlands and imported and redistributed textiles, metal, pepper, tobacco, coffee, sugar, and manufactured goods.

A ninth-century Chinese document mentions Po-pa-li [Berbera], as the Horn of Africa was called during this period.[4] Chinese Sung dynasty pottery (960-1279 A.D.) has been found at Mogadishu and probably was traded into the area from the Arabian peninsula.[5]

In the tenth century, Arabs established the commercial cities of Merca and Brava on the east coast, which soon began to rival Zeila and Mogadishu in the international trade network. Ibn Battuta visited the trading entrepots of Zeila and Mogadishu in 1331.[6] According to Ming dynasty records, in 1422 envoys from China were sent to Mu ku tu su [Mogadishu] and to Chu pu, a city near Mogadishu. Subsequently envoys from these cities visited the court of Yeng Lo, in 1427 A.D. Precious stones, coral, and amber, as well as giraffes, lions, zebras, leopards, ostriches, and white pigeons, were mentioned as being traded to the Chinese.[7] The nineteenth century saw a commercial boom for the East Coast of Africa, with European, American, and Zanzibarian merchants trading along the coast. During this period the Somalis exported ivory, textiles, ostrich feathers, hides, vegetables dyes, and oils.[8]

From the tenth century onwards, the Somali pastoralists expanded

17

southwards into their present-day territory through a series of gradual migrations. By the time of Ibn Battuta's visit in the fourteenth century, the original Arab populations of Zeila and Mogadishu were already Somalized. Ibn Battuta referred to the two cities' inhabitants as Barbara or Berbers to distinguish them from the Zinj or Zengi, the blacks, who inhabited the coast and hinterlands south of the Shabelle river.[9]

> I traveled from the city of Adan by sea for four days at the city of Zaila, the city of the Barbara....Their country is a desert extending for two months journey beginning at Zaila and ending at Magdashaw. Their animals are camels, and they also have sheep which are famed for their fat. The inhabitants of Zaila are black in colour and the majority of them are Rafidis....We sailed on from there for fifteen nights and came to Magdashaw which is a town of enormous size....The sultan of Magadashaw is, as we have mentioned, called only by the title of the Shaikh. His name is Abu Bar, son of shaikh Omar; he is by origin of the Barabara and he speaks in Maqdishi, but knows the Arabic language.

Sometime before the sixteenth century, most of the Zinj [Bantu-speaking peoples?] living south of the Shabelle river in present-day Somalia were displaced into Kenya by the Oromo expansion. The continual expansion of the Somali pastoralists southwards eventually pushed the Oromo into Ethiopia.[10]

Because of the complex historical migrations within Somalia and the long-standing international trade networks in which Somalia played an important role, the world of everyday experience in Somalia is not monolithic but is made up of several broad socioeconomic complexes. Somalia can be divided into three zones: the northern region, the inter-river area between the Shabelle and Juba rivers, and the coastal trading centers. Pastoral nomads live in the country's northern and central range-lands, where they herd camels, goats, and sheep. Sedentary and semi-sedentary farmers produce grain, cotton, and fruit in the southern arable lands between the Juba and Shabelle rivers. The coastal towns serve, as they have for centuries, as the principal centers for internal and inter-national trade.

The population of the northern region is fairly homogeneous. The northern pastoralists known as Samaale constitute over 50 percent of the population of Somalia. In the interriver area, the population is more heterogenous. One important group includes the two major sedentary-herding clans, known collectively as the Saab. Along the rivers there are also sedentary agriculturalists, who claim descent from the original inhabitants of the land, the groups which lived in the area prior to the sixteenth century. These groups include the Kabole, Rer Issa, Makanne, and the Shabelle, who live along the Shabelle river, and the Wa Gosha, Boni, and Gobawein, who live along the Juba river.[11] In the last quarter of the nineteenth century, when antislavery campaigns along the Benaa-dir coast began in earnest, these river settlements were augmented by groups of runaway slaves who established themselves along the lower

Juba and Shabelle rivers.[12] The heterogenous populations of the coastal cities constitute a third cultural zone. The term *Benaadir* was first used by the Arabs for the commercial ports along the southern Somali coast from Cadale to Baraawe.[13] These Somali cities have strong historical ties to the coastal mercantile centers which extend from Somalia to Mozambique.

Cutting across the three regions are groups of people who have been historically attached to the northern, interriver, and coastal populations in a client relationship. These are the Sab groups, who are the professional artisans in metal and leather. They include the Tumal, Yibir, and Midgan. The Tumal are blacksmiths who engage in the production of arms and domestic tools. The Yibir are leatherworkers who fashion amulets, shields, sandals, and other leather products. The Midgan, a term now prohibited by law in Somalia, are hunters, medical practitioners, barbers, and hairdressers.[14]

The northern pastoral culture clearly dominates Somalia, and it is not surprising in studies of Somali arts that an emphasis has always been placed on the artistic expression of this northern majority. Furthermore, because of the important place that poetry holds within the nomadic culture, scholarship has naturally focused on an exegesis of their verbal arts.

In 1854, the English Arabist and explorer Richard Burton traveled through Somalia. He commented about the pervasiveness of the poetic traditions:[15]

> The country teems with "poets, poetasters, poetitos, poetaccios": every man has his recognized position in literature as accurately defined as though he had been reviewed in a century of magazines—the fine ear of this people causing them to take the greatest pleasure in harmonious sounds and poetical expressions, whereas a false quantity or a prosaic phrase excite their violent indignation.

The verbal arts of the north include a number of poetic genres. *Gabay, jiifto,* and *geeraar* are classical verse composed by men. *Gabay* and *jiifto* poetry address serious political, philosophical, and religious issues. The *geeraar* are poems about war which were chanted to raise the morale of warriors and ridicule one's adversaries. *Buraambur* poetry is a women's art form. These poems explore themes relating to marriage, death, friendship, and other serious life concerns. Unlike men's classical poetry, *buraambur* poems are often recited to musical accompaniment. *Heello* is a relatively recent genre, which was first introduced in 1954. Ostensibly love poems, *heellooyin* also address sensitive contemporary political topics in veiled speech.[16]

Among the northern nomads, the classical men's poetry not only is an important form of artistic expression, but it figures heavily in the political arena. Poetry is the primary medium whereby an individual or a segment can present a case most persuasively. The Somali pastoral poet composes verse on all important clan occasions. Through his poetry he expresses and formalizes the important issues of the age. When a poem composed in the past is recited today, it often is accompanied by an introductory prose segment which explains to the contemporary audience the historical events which the poet recorded in his verse.

In addition to poetry's function as a chronicle of events and attitudes of a specific age, people perceive that poetry has the power to affect social relationships. It can be used to move people to undertake a vendetta or to sustain an existing feud, or to bring a feud under control. Poetry thus affects in a very direct way the process of social interaction.[17]

Authors of these classical genres have never been anonymous. Andrzejewski noted:

> It was indicative of the high position held by poets of the public forum that their oral poems enjoyed the protection of an unwritten copyright law. Anyone who memorized someone else's poem and wanted to recite it afterwards was under a strict obligation to remember the text accurately to the best of his ability and to reproduce it faithfully at each recital, for he was considered to be a channel of communication and in no way a co-author with the original poet. Another provision of this copyright law was the reciter had to give the name of the poet at each recital, and its omission or a knowing misappropriation was treated as a serious breach of the ethical code.

This point is a particularly important one to emphasize in the study of African art. Much of the early scholarship on the African artist presumed that the artist remained anonymous in his own culture. The classical poetry tradition of Somalia offers a clear example of specific authorship in African oral arts.

Among pastoral peoples, the richness and variety of their oral arts overshadow their visual-art production. Their material objects display an economy of form that is appropriate to peoples who move frequently and for long distances. These functional objects of everyday life, i.e., the milk jugs, the woven mats, the weapons, the camel bells, and the nomadic houses, are all carefully crafted.

The nomadic house, the *aqal,* is beehive-shaped and constructed of a wooden skeletal armature covered with layers of mats. The interior height is generally between four and seven feet. Two beds lie on either side of the entrance, and around the floor are various containers for water and milk. Other small utensils are stored in the framework of the house.[18] Water and milk vessels are often woven from fiber and then proofed with wax or fat and steeped in an infusion of acacia bark. Finely carved wooden beakers for serving coffee, milk, or water and wooden milk jugs are standard equipment in the nomadic household. Engraved ostrich-egg containers decorated with leather straps are also used as water containers.[19]

Women weave a variety of mats, which are used as camel blankets, as exterior coverings for the nomadic house, and as carpets and mattresses for the interior. This last category is generally more finely woven and is often elaborately decorated with multicolored designs. The mats are constructed of five or more individually fashioned strips, which are sewn together to form the finished mat.[20]

Headrests, *barkin,* are used as pillows. According to Puccioni, there are two different types of headrests: one type is used by men, the second by women. The men's headrest is generally narrower at the bottom than at the top, and it is consequently rather unstable. The type used by women is square and sits firmly on the ground. Both are ornamented with engravings.[21]

Pastoralists are known as great warriors. In the male ethos, a warrior's spears, knives, shields, and horse gear are his most important possessions. They are made by professional ironworkers and leatherworkers, who trade with the pastoralists in exchange for milk, butter, and other goods.

Beyond its purely utilitarian function, a domestic object can take on additional meanings. Headrests, for example, are standard items of furniture throughout the nomadic community. Yet, they also are seen as having a protective function and figure in a popular belief that states that if a person's head is elevated above the ground during sleep, scorpions and snakes will not attack him. Men's headrests also function as symbols. Men are charged with guarding the herds at night. The instability of their headrests prevents them from falling into a deep sleep, and the headrest itself has become the tangible symbol of vigilance.[22] Cerulli noted that the headrest also plays a role in nuptial ceremonies. It is under the bride's headrest that the groom places the *tubash,* the defibulation price. The morning after the marriage is consummated, women enter the bride's *aqal* to confirm the evidence of her virginity. The bride then lifts the headrest from the marriage bed and takes this sum of money which she uses to purchase an amber necklace, the symbol of her new status.[23]

Ordinary domestic objects also provide some of the key imagery for the pastoral poet. Poetry illuminates the social and political worlds of the nomad while drawing on everyday objects and experiences for its imagery. It is a reflexive activity from which a larger truth can be created. To understand the allusions in pastoral poetry, it is crucial to have the knowledge of the everyday world of the nomad and the material objects in this world. For example, the milk vessel, whether of basketry or wood, is a standard container in the nomadic household. In an excerpt from a poem by Gabai Shinni, the poet uses the image of a vessel brimming with milk as a metaphor for a proud man:

> When fortune places a man even on the mere hem of her robe
> He quickly becomes overbearing.
> A small milking vessel when filled to the brim soon overflows.[24]

The production of certain household objects can also become an occasion for performance, in which both the objects and songs play a crucial role. Women weave the elaborately decorated mats which are used as furniture in the nomadic household. Upon the completion of one of these mats, the women perform it. They hold the mat aloft and dance it while singing its praises and praises for its creators. One of the songs associated with this performance reads:

> O weaving reeds, may you never be poverty stricken.
> May you never be taken for sale in the market.
> May none be ignorant of your maker.
> May no unworthy man ever tread on you.[25]

In the performance, attention is drawn to the mat as an artistic product, and recognition is given to the artist-weavers who act as the dancers of the mat. Thus, the authorship of the object is publicly proclaimed, and this recognition, though less formal and less enduring than that given to the classical poet, echoes the pastoralists' concern for recognizing the creative person within their society.

In contrast to those in the nomadic north, the quantity and quality of the visual arts in the coastal cities are immediately apparent. Multi-storied Arabian-style houses of coral stone dot the horizon. These houses often have intricately carved lintels, doors, and windows, and the interiors are furnished with elaborately decorated storage chests, chairs, and beds.

The style of Somali coastal carving forms the northern extension of the Azanian-style complex which extends from Cape Guardafui in Somalia to Sofala in Mozambique.[26] Grottanelli noted that certain motifs, i.e., the twelve-petal rosette and four-petal "aster" encased in a quadrangular frame, appear frequently on Somali architectural members and household furniture. Carved wooden combs and spoons for serving roasted coffee beans also carry similar motifs. These same motifs frequently appear on the architecture of Lamu island and on architectural monuments in southern Tanzania. This Azanian style is part of an old artistic tradition that has persisted for centuries on the coast of East Africa.[27]

The furnishings in the urban household can also take on added significance in certain ritual contexts. Among some groups in the cities, when a newborn child is first introduced into the household, a special ritual is performed. During this ritual the child is carried through each room, and the same household objects which are thought of in everyday experience as merely furniture become symbols of kinship relationships. For example, pointing to a chair, the elder says, "Child, this is the chair of your grandfather." In this ritual context, the abstract principles of kinship are given material form.

Most of the silver and gold work is done on the coast, and there is a guild of silver- and goldsmiths, who are considered an artisan caste.[28] But little has been published about the identity of the jewelers and the history of the tradition. Like the wood-carving motifs, jewelry designs seem to have had their original inspiration from Arabian and Indian prototypes. Necklaces, bracelets, earrings, armlets, silver-covered sandals, earpicks, and cosmetic containers are made by jewelers in the urban centers and are traded to groups throughout Somalia.

On ceremonial occasions, women wear silver bracelets and anklets, as well as gold and silver earrings and necklaces. This jewelry serves as the symbol of the wealth of the family, and particular types, such as the wedding necklaces, indicate a woman's marital status. Both men and women also wear elaborately wrought gold, amber, and silver *hersi*. More than just symbols of wealth, the *hersi* function as protective amulets which contain appropriate verses from the Koran.

Cloth production is an important industry in the coastal areas. The cotton fabric which is known commercially as Benaadir cloth is woven by men. The uncut fabric measures about fourteen yards in length, and it is generally brightly colored and often striped. Reds, yellows, and blues predominate.[29]

In 1330, Ibn Battuta made reference to a thriving cloth industry at Mogadishu:[30] "In this place are manufactured the woven fabrics called after it [Mogadishu] which are unequalled and exported from it to Egypt and elsewhere." Prior to the nineteenth century, raw cotton was imported from India. In the early nineteenth century, American merchants introduced an inexpensive mass-produced cotton fabric into Somalia. Somali producers responded to this threat to the local cloth industry by starting cotton plantations in the area between the Juba and Shabelle rivers, thus creating a viable local source for the raw material and meeting the challenge from the imported cloth.[31]

In the area between the Juba and Shabelle rivers, the verbal and visual arts have developed differently from those in the north, and they demonstrate a symbiotic mingling of pastoral and agricultural traditions. The social structure of this area is more hierarchical than that of the northern pastoralists, and one form of verbal arts that is more expressive of this pattern and is associated exclusively with the semisedentary agriculturalists is formulaic praise-singing performed by professionals, the *laashin*. The songs embody the history of the lineage and are performed at public festivals and at weddings. In form they are reminiscent of genealogical singing in other areas of sub-Saharan Africa.

The *Istun* stick fight is performed during the celebration of the Somali solar new year, which generally falls at the beginning of August. At Afgooye, the organization of this festival is based on the traditional moiety division of the clan which founded the town in the sixteenth or seventeenth century. Each moiety holds a *shir*, or procession, of adult males, who sing the history of the moiety. Following the procession, two teams of young men drawn from the two moieties engage in mock battles, the stick fights. Young men and women sing pithy couplets praising their own teams and chiding the opposition. In the formal organization of this festival, in the songs, and in the stylized dance gestures, the performance makes explicit the history of the town and its alliances and divisions.[32]

The material culture of the south is the least studied in Somalia, and we are almost entirely dependent on Puccioni's brief descriptions for any information on the southern traditions. The architecture of the agricultural communities differs from both the nomadic houses and the Arabian-style coral stone houses on the coast. The southern houses, *mundille,* are single-room circular buildings constructed of mud and wattle. The structure of the conical roof resembles an umbrella, with a center pole up to nine feet tall which supports a roundel. The roof beams fan out from the center pole like the spokes of an umbrella. Poles, beams, the roundel, and doors often are carved with geometric patterns in the coastal Azanian style. Occasionally the poles and beams also carry representations of household objects and animals.[33]

Ceramic vessels are manufactured in the interriver area and on the coast. Puccioni made a distinction between the coastal pottery and the interriver forms. He felt that the coastal pottery had an Arabian origin, while the southern pottery was indigenous to the area, and he attributed its development to the Bantu-related groups. Storage jars, incense burners, lamps, and charcoal burners are typical terra cotta products. Puccioni's descriptions of the pottery traditions are vague. He stated that the vessels are thrown on a wheel and fired in shallow pits. Men are the potters, but women sometimes help in the firing process.[34] Yet, it is not clear whether his descriptions of the division of labor and the technology were accurate for both coastal and southern pottery manufacture.

Wooden stools, drums, and flutes are associated almost exclusively with the southern region. Based on his observations of the woodworking tools and technology, Puccioni hypothesized that the southern wood-carving tradition owed more to the former Zinj inhabitants of the region than to any outside influences.[35]

Masking traditions, unknown on the coast and among the northern pastoralists, also have been reported in the south. Clark published notes on a hunters' association among the Eelay in the interriver area which uses goatskin face masks. The Eelay are part of the semisedentary Rahanweyn clan. During one ceremony, two dancers appeared, each wearing a mask which was daubed with white paint around the eyes and nose and had a moustache of goathair attached to the chin. They wore red headbands to which black feathers were attached, and necklaces of dried camel dung. The dancers were accompanied by a drummer, and a women's chorus who chanted and clapped the rhythms.[36]

The Wa Gosha, who live on the Juba river, also have carved wooden face masks. They are painted black, with additions of shells to indicate teeth and eyes. Fiber is added for hair and beards. These masks are used in rainmaking and curing rites.[37]

Many questions remain unanswered about the arts of Somalia. Although nomadic poetry is well documented, there is a lacuna in the scholarship on coastal and southern verbal art forms. But more critically, little research has been conducted on the visual arts, although there are substantial collections of Somali materials in museums and private collections. The range of forms, their regional distribution and context, the identity and role of the artisans, the technology of manufacture, and the stylistic and formal relationships between Somali arts and those produced in Ethiopia and Kenya are questions which need to be addressed. The exhibition *Somalia in Word and Image* can be only a beginning, and it is hoped that it will whet scholars' interest in the arts of Somalia.

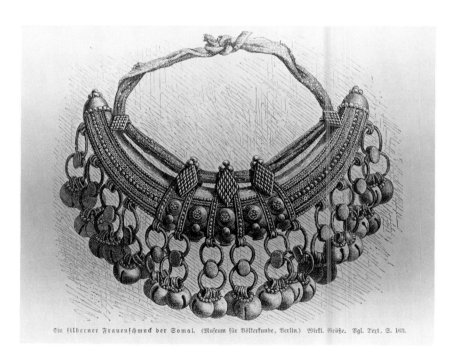

Porte Koran. From F. Ratzel, *Völkerkunde,* p. 163. Zweiter Band, Bibliographisches Institut, Leipzig und Wien, 1895. The Porte Koran is referenced as being from the Museum für Wölkerkunde, Berlin.

Ein silberner Frauenschmuck der Somal. (Museum für Völkerkunde, Berlin.) Wirkl. Größe. Vgl. Text. S. 163.

Soumali armé de la sagaie et du bouclier.

SOMALI carrying a shield and a spear. From C. Guillain, *Voyage à la Côte Orientale d'Afrique,* Plate 21. E. Ciceri Lith., Vayot, and A. Bertrand, Editor, Paris, 1856. Figure, courtesy Cambridge University Library.

SOMALI VERBAL
AND
MATERIAL ARTS

Said Sheikh Samatar

Those acquainted with the language and culture of the pastoral Somalis will have appreciated the preeminent, sometimes sinister role which poetry plays in Somali life and thought.[1] Whereas in the industrialized West, poetry—and especially what is regarded as serious poetry—seems to be increasingly relegated to a marginal place in society, Somali oral verse is central to Somali life, involved as it is in the intimate workings of people's lives. Indeed, the one feature which unfailingly emerges even from a casual observation of Somali society is the remarkable influence of the poetic in the Somali cultural and political scene. The Somalis are often described as a "nation of bards" whose poetic heritage is a living force intimately connected with the vicissitudes of everyday life.

In seeking to account for the unusual hold of the poetic art on the Somalis, British and Italian social anthropologists and folklorists would look to environmental factors for clues. The life of Somali nomads, it is said, is a life of wandering and danger, devoted as it is to eking out a living in a demanding environment. In the great boredom and bleakness of their surroundings, the theory goes, the Somali nomads turn to their poetry, the one thing that does not cost them anything and provides them with drama and entertainment. According to this view, without the twin inspiration of their faith and verse, the Somalis would waste themselves in fury and desperation.

Admittedly, that is a quaint argument, though it may have some merits. Environmental bleakness per se hardly makes for poetry and poetic creativity. To interpret the lyric verse of the Somali pastoralists merely as a survival mechanism, a feeble and self-pitying cry designed to mitigate life's cruelties to man, is to miss the significance of the poetic craft in Somali society.

What, then, makes the poetry such a pervasive force in Somali society? To the Somalis the question is not so difficult to answer: poetry is the medium whereby an individual or a group can present a case most persuasively. The pastoralist poet, to borrow a phrase, is the public-relations man of the clan, and through his craft he exercises a powerful influence in clan affairs. Unlike Western poetry, which appears to be primarily a concern of a group of professionals dealing with, more often than not, a subject matter intended for the members of what seems a small, highly literate section of society, Somali pastoral verse is a living art affecting almost every aspect of life. Its functions are versatile, concerned not only with matters of art and aesthetics but also with questions of social sig-

27

nificance. It illuminates culture, society, and history.

In addition to its value as the literary and aesthetic embodiment of the community, Somali poetry is a principal medium of mass communication, playing a role similar to that of the press and television in Western societies. Somali poets thus, like Western journalists and newsmen, have a great deal to say about politics and the acquisition of political power. Because it is the language and the vehicle of politics, the verse that Somali poets produce is an important source of Somali history, just as the printed and televised word performs a similar function in the West.

It is the duty, for example, of the Somali pastoral poet to compose verse on all important clan events and to express and formalize in verse the dominant issues of the age—in short, to record and immortalize in verse the history of his people. And since the poet's talents are employed not only to give expression to a private emotion but also to address vital community concerns, his verse reflects the feelings, thoughts, and actions of his age.

The widespread community acceptance of the validity and efficacy of the poetic medium in social relations seems to stem from pastoral notions of feud and vendetta, especially the institution of *godob*. Among the various components that constitute the *godob* institution is the concept of speech vendetta—the notion that certain kinds of oratorical forms can be used for slander. To borrow a pastoralist phrase, poetic orations serve the potent task of either "violating or ennobling the sour" of a person or a group. When poetic formulations are used to wound someone's honor, a case of *godob* has been generated. The resulting grievance, if it is not redressed or offset by a counter poetic formulation, becomes grounds for violent hostility between persons or groups. And indeed, poetic slander has been the source of many a lethal interclan feud, for an insult or slander in poetry is considered in pastoral sanctions to have the same effect on the victim as a physical assault.

By the same token, the power of poetry can be (and is) used to reconcile two parties who are on the brink of war. Thus, in pastoral ethos, poetry is both the instrument to precipitate and sustain feuds and a principal means to bring feuds under control.

The second point making for the power of poetry in pastoral culture concerns the monopolistic nature of the craft. In pastoral society as in others, a relatively small number of people are endowed with the talent to compose high-quality verse—artistic genius hardly comes in abundant supply. As a result, the inaccessibility of the art to most members of the population makes it a scarce commodity, the exclusive tool of a favored few. The few, aware of the high demand of their skill and the privileged status which their trade confers on them, use their talents to maximize their social and political influence. Hence, the pastoral bard occupies a prominent place in society. Lord of the desert and the dominant voice of the clan, he is envied by his less endowed kinsmen. It is his coveted task to articulate and register in verse the concerns of the community and the noteworthy deeds of his people.

Given its regular features of alliterative and metrical structure, Somali pastoral verse is easy to memorize, far more so than prose can be. The significance of this fact is easy to grasp if we bear in mind that in an oral culture where writing is unknown, except by a few roving holy men, the only libraries of reference materials men have are their memories. Thus, the events which are truly memorable in clan affairs are committed to verse, first so as to underscore their importance, and second, so they can better be remembered. In this way versification enables the pastoralists not only to transmit information across considerable distances but also to record it for posterity. Hence, Somali pastoral verse functions both as a social communicator and as an archival repertoire.

Somali society is largely nomadic, with people constantly on the move to find fresh pasture and water for their herds of camel, cattle, sheep, and goats. That necessitates frequent dispersals and comingling of people as the clans respond to the erratic patterns of yearly rainfall. At least once every other year, when climate permits, the clans reassemble to settle outstanding issues, and often to hold poetic contests. Each clan presents its best poets and their retinue of poem memorizers *(Hafida yaal)*, whose task is to disseminate and preserve for posterity the texts of the master poets who do verbal battle with opponent poets of rival clans.

The contest is overseen by a hoary panel of elderly arbitrators universally recognized for their mastery of the art of literary criticism and for rendering impartial decisions. Prizes are given to the best half-dozen or so poets, and the prizes offered on a particular occasion depend on the size and wealth of the assembling clans, ranging from a token gift such as a dagger or a piece of cloth to half a dozen camels. Needless to say, the latter represents considerable financial reward. But the greatest incentive for pastoral poets to compose stems from the honor and prestige that they derive from the exercise of their talents.

The change over the past forty years of a great many Somalis from nomadic to urban life and the consequent growth of written literature have not diminished the appeal of the oral arts. Contrary to the common misconception that an oral literature disappears as soon as a written one makes its appearance, the writing of Somali for the first time in 1972 has not adversely affected the oral traditions. If anything, it has expanded their influence. To cite a few examples, the word *layli,* meaning school "homework" in the urban context, is the word for "breaking" a young camel for burden bearing. The lover in a modern drama based on a written text says that because of unrequited love, he is stricken with *dukaan,* the disease which camels in drought suffer from. Similarly, the singer of a popular song likens the tender sentiment which he has toward the lady he loves to what, in the metaphor of oral poetry, a camel feels toward her suckling baby: "Groan in agony of love," he sings, "like a camel whose baby is unjustly sequestered away from her." For her part, the woman poet admonishes her suitor to give her "fine pastures, and pat her gently on the udder so she'd give milk." The jealous husband, in his bitter sarcasm and ridicule, points out to his wayward wife that it is only the "camel which enjoys being milked by two men at the same time, and that not only in all seasons, but solely when she is in full lactation." "Anything else of the feminine gender shared by two men is soon debased," he moralizes.

The term *warfin* (express mail delivery) is derived from the same root as *waraf* (slingshot), the old weapon used to pelt the destructive birds which peck on camels' humps. Similarly, the scholar acknowledges a debt every time he uses the word *raadraa* (to trace something), which is used to denote the word *research.* The word is employed by the nomads when tracking lost animals or when tracing stock thieves. The Marxists, too, have a debt to the nomads for appropriating *hugaanka,* a pastoralist term for leading a camel by the rope, as their modern term for their bureau of ideology (Hugaanka Ideologiyadal).

Moreover, the introduction in urban centers of modern media of communication such as the radio and motor transport have greatly enlarged the reach of oral poetry. Somalia has two radio stations, one in the city of Hargeisa in the north and the other in Mogadishu in southern Somalia. In addition, there are weekly Somali services on radio of foreign capitals, for example, in Cairo, Rome, London, Moscow, and Peking. Thanks to Japanese and Korean mass production of cheap, portable transistor shortwaves, which have made their way to the Somali countryside, the nomads tune in regularly to these radio stations to keep in touch with world developments and to avail themselves of literary productions broadcast especially from the Somali national radios and the BBC. Pastoral poets participate in these programs by sending their works with poem-memorizers, who travel on lorries to the cities, where the poems are tape-recorded, evaluated, and, if deserving, broadcast over radio. Thus, it is a common, if amusing, thing to come upon a group of nomads huddled excitedly over a short-wave transistor, engaged in a heated discussion of the literary merits of poems that have just been broadcast while they keep watch over their camel herds grazing nearby.

Somali poetry, surely one of the principal achievements of the Somalis, has at long last received the kind of serious academic attention that it rightfully deserves. What so far has escaped the notice of foreign scholars—and hence makes this project distinctive—is the intimate connection between Somali visual and poetic arts, enabling these two elements of the culture to nourish and sustain each other as they enhance the Somalis' daily experience. The connection between the two realms of art stems from a complex set of interactive, underlying principles (moral, philosophical, aesthetic, utilitarian) which shapes the creation, use, and philosophy of both. Somali artists (both visual and poetic) do not create just for the sake of creating or for pleasure; they create for a reason. The occasion that prompts, for example, a poet to compose verse is socially significant, e.g., reconciling two hostile clans which are on the brink of war, through a poetic appeal. The best works of pastoral masters such as the Sayyid Muhammad Abdille Hasan (the mad mullah of British history), Salaan Arrabay, Qamaan Bulhan, and Ali Duuh is a committed verse. The Sayyid composed his 120 pieces (which the Somalis consider immortal) to appeal to his fellow countrymen to support his nationalist struggle against British colonialism, to mobilize public opinion for the cause, to discredit (through poetic diatribes) his enemies, and to enhance his own position. In short, he used his poetry as a formidable political weapon. Salaan Arrabay's best work, "O Kinsman, Stop the War," was, as the title implies, a poetic appeal to bring an end to a chronic virulent feud between two rival sections of his Isaaq clan. Tradition has it that the poet on his horse stood between the massed opposing forces and, with a voice charged with drama and emotion, chanted the better part of the day until the men, smitten with the force of his delivery, dropped their arms and embraced one another.

This and countless other examples (which space will not permit us to go into) illustrate the principle that while a pastoral poet may occasionally compose to give expression to a private inspiration, his ultimate concern is utilitarian: to inform, persuade, or convince a body of kinsmen of the merits of whatever task he seeks to accomplish.

As with the poet, so it is with the maker of material objects. Each carved or woven article, as the collection plainly demonstrates, is never an end in itself, but is rather a means to a larger cause or truth. Each object in the gallery of woodwork and woven material—the porridge bowls, spoons, milk jugs, baskets, headrests, camel bells, and watering troughs—represents a specific utilitarian function. Because their primary objective is functional, they are simple in design, lacking the ornate and complex intricacy of art for pleasure only, yet possessing an elegance and a grace in their simplicity. Even the large variety of decorative necklaces and beads which on surface appearance seem to have been created purely for aesthetic effects are in fact designed to make an important commentary on social relations. Thus, the kind of necklace a woman wears signifies her age and social status. As a child, she wears one kind of beads or necklace; as a teenager, another; as a young woman of marriage age, still another; and finally, as a grown woman with children, still another set. A woman wearing a ponderous set of golden beads wants to show to the world not only the wealth of her lineage but also the costly bridewealth a prospective candidate for her marital hand would have to provide; while by another set of beads, she signifies her willingness to entertain men with sexual favors.

If the utilitarian principle underlies the creation and appeal of Somali poetic and visual arts, their value in society rests on different but mutually reinforcing functions. The power of poetry, as we have seen, rests on its regulatory function of the politcal relations among the clans, that of visual art on mediating social relations; that is to say, on formalizing the metaphor by which social behavior is legitimated. For example, the vast majority of Somali artifacts whose original justification lies in their function as weapons, such as daggers, spears, axes, and other metal tools, are made by an artisan clan whose members specialize in making tools. Members of this clan occupy a superior economic position because of their monopolistic hold on industry, but a low social position which prohibits intermarriage with other clans. Their knowledge and skill in making tools are a badge of their social standing: thus, in a curious way economic success limits social status. The underlying rationale of this seemingly irrational sanction is to discourage the kind of grasping greed and unyielding acquisitiveness which accompanies the accumulation of material goods referred to as capitalism in the West. Thus, Somali visual art reflects the egalitarian anticapitalist temper of pastoralism in the way that oral poetry performs a similar function. To speak of the anticapitalist temper of pastoralism is not to suggest that the nomads are indifferent to material possessions and the power and prestige which they confer. The nomads cherish their few belongings. But in a sparse material culture, an untempered spirit of acquisitiveness and the accompanying mentality of every man for himself would undermine the processes of mutual help and collective action necessary to survival in the desert.

By traditional sanction, this clan of craftsmen and artisans is barred from composing verse; this principle is expressed by the proverb "To possess two good things is to rob your brother." These craftsmen possess one good thing: as principal artisans, they wield vast economic power. To keep them from gaining political power also (and hence becoming robbers), they are barred by social norm from composing verse, the key instrument to sociopolitical power. Members of this clan, therefore, attach themselves as clients to noble clans who have the political power to protect them. Poets from noble lineages compose verse on behalf of the artisans to immortalize their contribution to the culture, while the artisans make the tools and crafts that the noble clans need to meet daily necessities.

In the south of Somalia, among the sedentary population, a related but significantly different oral tradition has developed, which reflects the more hierarchic social structure of this region. A feature of it is the technique of formulaic praise-singing, in honor of individuals or families, by professional performers, known as *laashin*. It typically occurs at public festivals or weddings. Often it is combined with the communal chanting of refrains, which accompanies processions celebrating particular groups. Laashins also function as repositories of traditional history, since allusions to their patrons' ancestral glories are an important part of their performance. They carry their art into the modern context by performing at political meetings or occasions such as the opening of a school, and introduce the topics of the day into their performances alongside allusions to events in past history.

LEATHER SHIELDS. From F. Ratzel, *Völkerkunde,* p. 167.
Zweiter Band, Bibliographisches Institut, Leipzig und
Wien, 1895. The shields are referenced as being from
the Christy Collection, London.

Lederne Schilde der Somal. (Christy Collection, London.) ⅛ wirkl. Größe. Vgl. Text, S. 163.

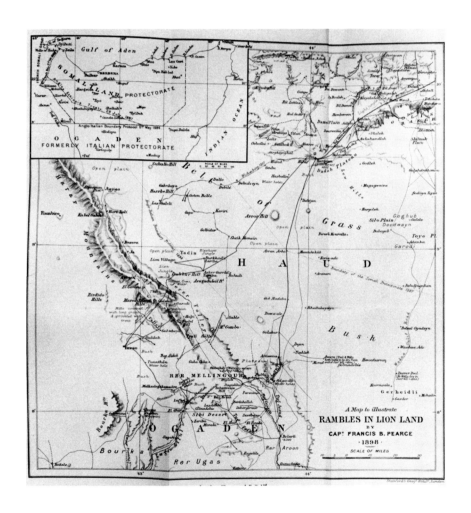

A Map to illustrate
RAMBLES IN LION LAND
BY
CAP.t FRANCIS B. PEARCE
·1898·
SCALE OF MILES

THE LITERARY CULTURE
OF THE SOMALI PEOPLE

B.W. Andrzejewski

Until some three decades ago, little was known outside Somalia about the literary achievements of its people, and even that scanty knowledge was shared by only a minute circle of scholars and people connected professionally with the Horn of Africa. This situation has now changed substantially: translations of Somali poems and stories are to be found in anthologies with pan-African and even world coverage,[1] and recognition has been given to the literature in reference works.[2]

This growth of interest is to a large extent part of the general awakening in Europe and North America to the cultural wealth of the developing countries, which so often used to be overlooked and undervalued, but other factors are also present in the Somali case. Among them are the direct aesthetic appeal and universal human interest of many of its themes, and the fact that the poetry of Somalia has some special characteristics which are highly relevant to the current debate on the mode of composition, memorization, and transmission of oral poetry.[3]

Before the 1950s, the Somali language was not used to any appreciable extent as a vehicle for written, as opposed to oral, literature. Some manuscripts of religious poems in Somali, written in the Arabic script, were found and later published by the Italian scholar Enrico Cerulli.[4] However, the composition and circulation of such manuscripts must have been very small, since none are extant, as far as I have been able to ascertain.

The almost total absence of written literature in that period stood in sharp contrast to the intensive artistic cultivation of the spoken word throughout the Somali-speaking territories. There was a thriving oral literature, which was truly oral in the sense that its composition, memorization, transmission, and dissemination all took place without recourse at any stage to writing or any other technology of communication and memory storage. Many of its genres were such as are commonly found in oral literatures all over the world: poetic texts for work and dance songs,[5] tales and anecdotes for adults, and animal fables for children.[6] In addition, it had historical narratives concerned with the deeds of prominent members of the community,[7] and legends of the Muslim holy men who were venerated on account of their piety and the miracles attributed to their intercession.[8] But there was a group of genres, all poetic, which had some unusual features and were the most valued part of oral literature within Somali society. This type of poetry, which it seems appropriate to call classical verse, was structurally very complex and sophisticated in sentiment; it was poetry of the public forum and was used as a mass medium of communication and a repository of knowledge about the past.[9] The poets who practiced it frequently commented on public affairs, whether of their immediate community or of the whole nation, and endeavored, sometimes very successfully, to influence the course of events by molding public opinion and stirring their listeners to action.

In precolonial Somalia, poets often acted as spokesmen for clans, territorial groups, or confederacies, presenting their views in poetic form and using praise, flattery, censure, derision, or even downright verbal abuse as the occasion demanded. They incited people to war or counseled peace, and they rejoiced over the defeat of an enemy or lamented over the wrongs done to their own people; but sometimes they acted as individuals, defending their own actions against criticism or leveling accusations against their opponents. Poetry was often used in disputes concerning marriage, divorce, or broken engagements, matters which were far from being treated as purely private, since successful marriages cemented interclan alliances and involved reciprocal obligations, while divorce and broken engagements could put a strain on such relations or could injure the reputation of one of the parties if any socially unacceptable behavior was revealed in a dispute. A great deal of smoothing over and face saving was achieved through poetry, but on the other hand, defamatory poetry was often the source of feuds and violence. Poets looked after their own prestige very carefully, and by custom were allowed to boast as much as they wished—not only about themselves but about their horses, which were particularly valued in Somali society; a horse which excelled in beauty, speed, or battle skills brought true glory to its master.

It was indicative of the high position held by poets of the public forum that their oral poems enjoyed the protection of an unwritten copyright law. Anyone who memorized someone else's poem and wanted to recite it afterwards was under a strict obligation to remember the text accurately to the best of his ability and to reproduce it faithfully at each recital, for he was considered to be a channel of communication and in no way a coauthor with the original poet. Improvisations, substitutions, or deletions, if made willfully, were regarded as dishonest, and if they were unintentional were tolerated only as lapses due to the frailty of human memory. Another provision of this copyright law was that the reciter had to give the name of the poet at each recital, and its omission, or a knowing misattribution, was treated as a serious breach of the ethical code.

Somali poetry is alliterative, and its rules require that in each line throughout a poem there should be either one or two words, depending on the length of the line, beginning with the same consonant or with a vowel, all vowels being considered to alliterate with each other. An example of how that is done is given in the poem below, where the alliterative consonant is *dh*. The poem is a lament over the poet's old age and a dignified plea for better treatment, for he proves by his skillful use of poetic language that he is still in full possession of his mental faculties. It is attributed to Raage Ugaas, a celebrated nineteenth century poet.[10]

Inta khayli dhuugyaha cas iyo, dheeg wiyil ah qaatay
E dhallaanka Aadnigu u baxo, sidatan lay dhawray
Kolkii hore ba dhererkii miyaa, dhabarkii soo gaabtay
Ma ka dhaxay dhawaaq uubatiyo, dheelmitaan gibin ah
Dhabbe reero qaadeen miyaa, laygu wada dhaafay
Ushan dhaabin mooyee hubkii, ma iska wada dhiibay
Raggaan dhalay raggu dhalay miyaa, dharabo ii diiday
Kuwi aniga ii dhaxay miyaa, dhimashaday dooni
Dhuuniga i siiyaay miyaa, sida dhallaan ooyey
Waxan dhawrsan jiray ceeb miyaa, igu dharaarowday

Once I wore a fine red-brown mantle and carried a rhinoceros-hide whip
I was looked upon with esteem as one among the best of humankind
But then my backbone grew short and shrank, did it not?
I even had to stop for a night's rest, did I not, when traveling a distance so short that shouting voices could have spanned it
I was passed and left behind on the way, was I not, by everyone along the route which trekking hamlets take
I had to give up carrying weapons altogether, did I not, except for a stick to support myself.
The men begotten by men whom I begot refused to lend me their aid
The women who were married to me wished me dead, did they not?
"Give me food!" I shouted, did I not—impatiently, like a child.
The shameful things against which I had guarded myself have now come upon me, clear as the light of day, have they not?

In classical poetry, the constraints of strict rules of scansion are added to those of alliteration. The scansion patterns depend on the length of syllables, with short syllables being treated as having one time unit and long ones as having two. The length of the syllable is determined by the length of its vowel or diphthong, and there are rules which determine the number of units in the line of each poetic genre. Taking the first two lines of the above poem as an example, with the long and short syllables marked according to their time units, it can be seen that the genre to which this poem belongs requires twenty units in a line, and that a break (caesura) occurs after the twelfth unit.

Inta khayli dhuugyaha cas iyo, dheeg wiyil ah qaatay
1 1 2 1 2 1 1 1 1 1 2 1 1 1 2 1
E dhallaanka Aadnigu u baxo, sidatan lay dhawray
1 1 2 1 2 1 1 1 1 1 1 1 1 1 2 2 1

The rules differ from genre to genre, and until recently they were not explicitly known or taught to aspiring poets; their correct use was a matter of intuition. Not until the 1970s were the principles of the scansion system discovered and worked out in broad outline by two Somali scholars, and detailed research is still in progress.[11]

The colonial partitions of Somalia which took place toward the end of the nineteenth century did nothing to destroy or even to diminish the practice of oral literature, and in fact the fierce resistance to foreign rule by the Somali Dervish Movement (1900-1921) stimulated the use of the poetry of the public forum and gave rise to many historical prose narratives. The leader of the Dervishes, Sayid Maxamed Cabdulle Xasan, was himself a poet of renown, and he used his poetry as a powerful weapon of propaganda, pleading in it for the support of his countrymen in the holy war against the foreigners, boasting about his own strength and victories, and threatening and pouring abuse on his enemies.[12] Many of his poems had clearly practical aims: in some he sent instructions to his subordinates explaining his strategical thinking; in others he sent proposals of alliance to neutrals or described his reprisals against defectors. His opponents were not merely the foreign powers but their Somali allies, as well, and among them poetic talent was not lacking, either, so that there was also a poetic war going on in which the two sides exchanged invective in verse, hurling accusations and urging each other's followers to change their allegiance. The poetry of this period is full of rejoinders and oral cross-references, and the most astonishing fact was that the poems crossed the enemy lines without much difficulty.

Although most of the poets, on both sides of the conflict, were concerned mainly with the conduct of the war, they remained faithful to their calling as artists. The formal skills of poetry continued to be highly cultivated, and so were the devices of poetic diction, such as the use of figurative language and the insertion of descriptive passages in poems with otherwise quite practical messages. That can be seen in the extract which follows from a poem known as *Jiinley,* that is, one alliterating in the sound *j,* composed by the Dervish leader.[13] The poem's practical aim was to bring disgrace on a seeming ally who at first had offered the Dervishes asylum in his territory and then apparently had changed sides under the threat of enemy reprisals. In his preamble, the poet praises and blesses his faithful court reciter, Xuseen Dhiqle, who is to learn the poem by heart and then "publish" it to others, who in their turn will transmit it to yet more listeners.

> O Xuseen, one must not utter contentious words, for you are my friend
> You did not leave me when the ignorant stampeded
> You did not go to Ethiopia's Emperor when your kinsmen moved away.
> The men who fawn upon infidels are people of Hell—
> I swear upon the whole Koran that they will go to Gehenna!
> You loaded your camels and came over to me when they defected to the British generals
> You are the kind of man who drinks no sour milk
> I have given up others, but as for you, you are my close friend
> And I count on you during the dry season of the year.
> A rosy cloud, a scud of white vapor, precipices of cloud flashing with lightning,
> Resounding thunder, flood-water running over the parched earth,
> The past night's repeated showers, noisy as the *jibin* bird

The heavy rain which fell, the longed-for rain of the spring,
Ponds brimming over, old camp-sites luxuriant,
Thorns become as tall as grass, thick undergrowth crackling—
I shall satisfy your needs as when one pours out salty water for a
    she-camel
And I shall entertain you with a poem as precious as a jewel.

The collapse of the Dervish Movement in 1921 was followed by one of the bleakest periods in Somali history. The depredations of the war had reduced many pastoralists to destitution, and the situation was made worse by the fact that large quantities of firearms had found their way into the nomadic interior and were now used in fratricidal warfare devoid of any ideological aspect. In these localized conflicts, poets again played their parts as spokesmen, whether instigating people to fight or counseling peace and appealing to the sentiments of a common culture and religion.[14]

Matters closer to personal and family affairs still concerned many people, however, and there were poems, for instance, justifying the poet's position in disputes about bridewealth payment or divorce. Love poetry was usually more of a eulogy of the poet's future or hoped-for bride than an intimate declaration of love, and was aimed at securing good relations with the girl and her family. A notable exception was that of Cilmi Bowndheri, who was believed to have died of love around 1941.[15] He was a baker in the northern port of Berbera, and fell in love with a girl whom he seems hardly to have known. His circumstances made it difficult to seek her hand in marriage, and she eventually was married to someone else, chosen for her by her family but willingly accepted by her. During the few years of his devotion to the girl, he composed many powerfully emotional poems, which brought him fame, and the story of his tragic love and death from grief has given rise to many oral prose narratives which have a wide circulation even to this day. In one poem he says of his love:[16]

At times I made light of it and I was free
Then suddenly I was shown her in a vision—she was the color of a
    lighted lantern
She must have become imprinted on my heart, for how else could I
    be so intoxicated by her?
Inside my breast she tick-tocks to me like a watch
At night when I fall asleep she comes to sport with me
But at early dawn she leaves me and turns into a rising pillar of dust.

The harshness of interclan warfare slowly abated with the passage of time into an uneasy peace under the various colonial administrations. In spite of the many negative aspects of this period, it transmitted to the coming generation a great deal of poetry of lasting value, marked rather by the refining of the older poetic tradition than by any innovations. But the Second World War and the years immediately after it brought many social changes to Somalia, one of the most fundamental being that the towns, which in the past had been small settlements with few inhabitants, grew in size, partly as a result of the development of trade and long-distance truck traffic, and partly from the expansion of central and local administration and education, which employed Somali personnel. Among the new town dwellers, it was the truck drivers, commercial entrepreneurs, clerks, interpreters, and teachers who occupied particularly important positions as agents of cultural change, for they welcomed all forms of innovation, and their ties with the traditional life of the rural interior were weakened as time went by.

It was among this group that a new genre of poetry arose, that of miniature love poems.[17] The poets took their formal models from the traditional light poetry, but the content was new, and its musical appeal was enriched by the use of tambourines, flutes, lutes, and later, other instruments such as accordions, which were portable and reasonably cheap. The theme of love was treated in an individualistic manner without too much concern for the niceties of traditional etiquette and the practice of premarriage negotiations between families and clans. The amorous verses were addressed either to real or to obviously fictitious men and women, and were characterized by a heightened lyricism and romantic hyperbole. Often the poems were recited at private parties, when the single lines or couplets were sung in turn by the company on the "string of pearls" principle; each short poem was self-contained artistically, and often achieved great compactness. This poetry was art for art's sake, at the opposite extreme from the poetry of the public forum, with its concern with matters of common interest.

Of the poetry of the public forum, those poems which were particularly favored by reciters and their audiences were preserved in people's memories for many years after the events which gave rise to their composition, but with the passage of time their allusions to once-topical situations tended to become obscure. That was remedied by the reciters' giving their own explanatory introductions in prose on the background of the poems, and sometimes, too, there were oral narratives in circulation which were linked to particular poems. The lives of the poets were always of interest to audiences, and since in Somalia everyone learns by heart the names of his forebears, it is possible for the descendant of a poet, by counting the generations, to place his ancestor fairly accurately in time. Thus, by various means Somalis created their own oral literary history and biography without recourse to writing, and in modern times that proved its value when Somali scholars turned their attention to writing down or tape-recording their national heritage.[18]

This work began in the 1950s, when a number of researchers started using their own unofficial methods of writing Somali, and at independence in 1960 the task of collecting oral texts and their background information was entrusted by the Somali government to the newly created Cultural Department of the Ministry of Education; its responsibilities later passed to the Academy of Arts and Sciences. When an official orthography was introduced in 1972, efforts were intensified to preserve the oral literature, and the results became available to a newly literate public who could now read the transcripts of oral texts which were published, often with introductions and annotations, as books or articles. Much of this material is also included in school textbooks for the teaching of Somali language and literature, and a number of B.A. dissertations in the field have been written by students at the Department of Somali Language and Literature at the National University of Somalia.

Although at the beginning of the 1950s Somali oral literature was still functioning in its pure form, developments already had begun which were to lead to its hybridization. These were the introduction of broadcasting and sound recording, and the use of written Somali as an aid to memory, though not yet at this time as a channel of communication. Since these new elements were all technological—for writing is certainly a technology—I use the term *techno-oral* to describe literature which retains many characteristics of its orality, yet is no longer fully oral, since it is backed by electronic devices and a limited use of writing.

Broadcasting in Somali started during the Second World War, mainly as an information service, but when peace came the number of radio sets increased rapidly, the hours of transmission were extended, and it was found that oral literature, especially sung poetry, provided excellent and easily obtainable broadcasting material. The 1960s saw a great expansion of tape recorder ownership, even in the rural interior, and an increasing circulation of the recorded poetry that was played for entertainment in private and in public.

Many poets now began to rely less on the traditional way of disseminating their works—recital, memorization, and further recital—and more on the radio and the tape recorder, the latter of which was soon found by reciters to be invaluable as a memory aid. Various private methods of writing were also sometimes used as aids to memory storage and composition. For instance three of the great poets of this period, Cali Xuseen, Cabdullaahi Qarshe and Cali Sugulle, used personal orthographies, but they did not publish their written texts at the time.

Techno-oral literature has not entirely replaced purely oral literature, which continues to be practiced even today, but it has reduced the importance of oral literature in the life of the nation. More people nowadays listen to poetry on the radio or on tapes than attend performances given by poets or reciters at parties and meetings; and though the old revered genres of the public forum are still used in the new electronic setting, they are less popular, especially in towns, than the modern poetry, whose origin can be traced to the miniature love poems which came into being in the 1940s. These had been found to be ideal radio material, for they did not have the divisive element of clan conflict which was so often present in the poetry of the public forum, and their lively musical accompaniments gave them an aura of modernity, which appealed particularly to the town population.[19] The special conditions imposed by a broadcasting studio enforced a change from the original "string of pearls" style of recitation, for it was impracticable and expensive to gather together the number of reciters that this style would entail. The performers were reduced to two, or even one, and as a result the poems became longer and acquired a unified structure. The vivid imagery and use of hyperbole typical of this poetry can be seen in this poem by Maxamed Good, "Shimbir," in which he exuberantly compares himself first to a young camel, then to a she-camel in milk, and finally to an encampment which is in flames after a burden camel has run loose among the log-fires:[20]

> Unless I see you I never get nourishment from sleep
> Like a young camel I bellow out to you
> I am to you as a she-camel is to her adopted calf when her own has
>   been killed.
> By running hard and with good luck I shall obtain you—
> I have made that my pledge.
> A camel burdened with curved hut-poles broke loose and ran over me
> He set me alight like a blazing log-fire.
> I saw you in a dream, adorned for a wedding-feast
> I cry out to you—have trust in me!

But this love poetry soon became politicized. The metaphoric and allusive language was well suited to fooling the foreign censors who at that time were trying to check the activities of those Somalis who were working towards independence, and it sometimes happened that an apparently harmless love lyric was easily decoded by Somali listeners into an attack on the authorities. Thus, a poem in dialogue, composed in 1956 by Xuseen Aw Faarax, in which a man and woman express their tender feelings and complain about people trying to keep them apart, actually referred to the alleged machinations of foreign politicians who were delaying the speedy unification of the Somaliland Protectorate with the UN Trusteeship Territory of Somalia, then under Italian administration.[21]

Some modern poems reflected the attitudes of their authors to events in the world outside Somalia, and a good example is a comment by Cabdullaahi Qarshe on the Berlin Wall. He uses the traditional Somali concept of *Nabsi,* the invisible power which levels out the inequalities of life and avenges arrogance, and which, as he says, "can be as slow as a tortoise, but which planes can never overtake." He draws his listeners' attention to the fact that this city, in which a nineteenth-century conference of colonial powers took place to divide Africa into zones of influence, was now itself divided:[22]

> Look at Berlin
> All of you look!
> A wall is splitting it—
> Look and be entertained!

The development of modern poetry was paralleled by the appearance of drama on the Somali cultural scene. It represented a syncretism of the purely Somali art of poetry with foreign techniques of portraying real life on a stage, and right from the start it was a great success with the public.[23] As far as can be ascertained, it came into existence around the time of the Second World War, the result, perhaps, of several influences, one of which would have been the sketches performed by soldiers in the so-called concerts organized by the British army in Somalia as entertainment for the troops. Another source of inspiration may have been the short plays put on in the schools for Somali boys and young men, set up first by the British military administration and then expanded in peacetime. Some people claim that amateur operatic performances by the Italian settlers in the south of Somalia also had an influence even before 1939.

At first the plays were short, of one or two scenes, but soon more elaborate plots were introduced to provide entertainment for a whole evening. The most important parts of the dialogue are in poetic form, conforming to the existing rules of alliteration and scansion, and they often are sung to the accompaniment of music like other modern poetry. The rest of the dialogue, which moves the plot along or concerns minor or comic characters, is in prose. Most plays are concerned with modern life situations, and the playwrights set themselves up as critics and reformers of contemporary society, using both satire and direct exhortation. Among the targets of their attacks have been resistance to modern education; forced marriage; the instability of marriages in towns and the consequent neglect of children; prostitution; tribalism; corruption; and superstitious practices such as spirit-possession dances. The actors are very rarely given scripts, and they learn their parts orally from the playwrights or from tapes, though many of the playwrights write their works down for their own benefit, as a memory aid. Scenes from live performances of the more popular plays are often broadcast, and whole plays are sometimes serialized.

Written literature in its pure form, that is, in which composition by the author and reception by the public both depend entirely on writing, is a recent innovation in Somalia. The private systems of writing which were in use between 1950 and 1972 were applied mainly to the transcription of oral literature; it was only when a national orthography in Latin script was established and Somali became the official language of the state that potential authors could be assured of a wide reading public. The introduction of Somali into schools as the medium of instruction, and the launching of adult urban and rural literacy campaigns, have encouraged a rapid growth of written literature, and even by 1975 there were substantial achievements to be noted in both poetry and prose.[24]

As far as poetry is concerned, that is of course not surprising, since it was already a highly cultivated art in its oral and techno-oral forms. The new poets had only to follow the existing rules of alliteration, scansion, and line division, for these were well suited to the demands of the printed page. They also used the established devices of poetic diction to the extent that it is impossible to tell from a printed text whether a particular poem belongs to written literature or is a transcript under dictation from a poetry reciter. The only innovative aspect is that some poems deal with themes which show a degree of familiarity with foreign cultures rarely found in oral or techno-oral poetry.

The writers of short stories and novels, on the other hand, did not take their formal models from the existing oral and techno-oral prose narratives, since these, though lively and interesting in their themes, were marked by a constant repetition of words and phrases used to introduce dialogue or indicate the passage of time, and were concerned mainly with the events described rather than with the background scenery or the emotional states of the characters. They were usually bare of stylistic ornamentation, but were enlivened in the telling by mimetic devices on the narrator's part, such as the imitation of nonspeech sounds, which could not be represented in a written form.

Instead, the new Somali prose writers turned for their models to short stories and novels in European languages, but only as regards form: the subject matter has remained firmly Somali. The realities of Somali life, past and present, whether in nomadic encampment, agricultural village, or modern town, are what interest both writers and readers, and great attention is paid to the accurate description of background detail and the depiction of recognizable emotional responses on the part of the characters.

Most of the new prose fiction appeared in serialized form in the literary pages of the national daily *Xiddigta Oktoobar (October Star)*, for the economic situation makes it difficult to publish more than a few works in book form. The authors have responded quickly to the demands of the serial form, some of them becoming masters of suspense, and it is a familiar sight to see an impatient crowd of readers outside a newspaper kiosk waiting to get the latest installment of their favorite serial of the moment.

In addition to suspense, there is the kind of detailed description and reflective thought that is usually absent from oral narratives, as can be seen in the following passage taken from a long short story, "Colaad iyo Caashaq" (War and Love) by Cismaan Caliguul,[25] which is set in precolonial Somalia. Beyddan, the heroine, and Buraale fall in love, but their respective clans are enemies in a fierce war. Risking his life, Buraale steals into the encampment of Beyddan's clan on a dark night, and they elope, riding together on a swift horse. As dawn approaches, the horse is tiring, and their tracks will in any case soon become visible to their pursuers. In this extract Beyddan is reliving the experience in later years as she talks to a young girl of the neighborhood:

> We rode on and on through the night in complete darkness—darkness which knew nothing of our troubles. I turned my head and there was the dawn pursuing us. We listened and the birds were chirping and twittering—they were pleased with the new day that was running toward them. How different was their situation from ours! They wanted the dawn to break quickly so that they could begin picking berries, and we wanted the dawn to linger behind so that we could escape beyond the territory of my clan under the cover of night.

Now we had come to an inhabited area, and the first thing we heard was the bleating of a goat. Suddenly a herd of gazelles was in front of us and the dawn was already bright. They mistook us for enemies stronger than themselves and sprinted away, but in truth we too were running from enemies stronger than ourselves. Soon we would be wishing that they might give us their speed!

The grass on which the rain had fallen the night before now spread its blades toward the sun for which it had been waiting, and the dew resting on the leaves of the trees took on the color of gold. The trees were pleased with the growing warmth and the sunshine, but all this was of no benefit to us, travelers who were passing by. Often what is noxious to you brings good to others!

These present trends give some indication of what is likely to happen in the next few decades in the Somali literary culture. Older oral literature preserved in annotated transcripts will continue to be read, and with the passage of time it will be valued ever more highly as the treasure hoard of the national heritage. As a living art, oral literature is already in a decline, which most probably will continue, so that eventually it will be limited to the poetic texts of work and dance songs, anecdotal narratives, and children's lore. In contrast, techno-oral literature has a very good chance not only of retaining its present position but even of expanding further, for three main reasons. The first is that Somali people take great pleasure in listening to vocal performances, especially if the performances are accompanied by music. The second lies in the gradual improvement of electronic channels of communication, not to mention the possibility of television being introduced in Somalia, as it already has been in Djibouti. The third reason lies in the existence of the Somali diaspora, especially in the more wealthy Arab countries. They maintain close links with their relatives at home, and there is a constant interchange of cassettes, often of a literary character. That is a particularly popular activity, since many members of the diaspora have had no opportunity to learn to read and write in Somali, even when they are fully literate in the language of their host country. It also provides a convenient chan- nel for poetic exchanges, very similar to those which in the old days were conducted through relays of poetry reciters.

Vigorous as it is, techno-oral literature is not likely to replace, or even overshadow, the now-healthy young tree that is written literature in Somalia. At the moment the main factor checking its further growth is an economic one. There are many valuable typescripts of poems, short stories, novels, and works of literary scholarship awaiting publication, and once there is some improvement in Somalia's material situation, we can expect a real flowering of written literature.

O death may your name perish!
Though in truth we are all on trek
Trudging in your direction

Excerpt from a poem by Cabdulqaadir Xirsi Yam Yam

Pass between Hargeysa and Buloxaar. Photo Abby
Thomas, 1967.

opposite Nomad on trek, Northern coast near Buloxaar.
Photo Abby Thomas, 1967.

above CAMEL loaded with provisions and water and milk containers. Northern Somalia. Photo Phoebe Ferguson, 1979.

below TWINED BASKET AND BASKET CARRIER. Middle Shabeelle. Photo Lee Cassanelli, 1977.

COILED BASKET WITH COVER, *dheel*. Northern Somalia. Smoked fiber and leather. H. 23cm. Collection F.C.C.U., Washington., D.C. These baskets are small enough to be carried by hand and are used for camel's milk and water. A new basket is sterilized and smoked with smoldering sticks, then proofed with wax or fat and steeped in an infusion of acacia bark which provides the tannin for proofing.

....Like a she-camel with a large bell
Come from the plateau and the region of the Upper Haud
The stifling heat of the sun is oppressive

Excerpt from a poem by an anonymous poet

above ORNAMENTAL OSTRICH EGG, *ugax goroyo.* Mogadishu. Shell, leather strappings and fringes and cowrie shells. D. 23cm. Collection Somali National Museum, Mogadishu. Sometimes used as water containers, ostrich eggs are traditionally presented to brides on their wedding day. They are symbols of good luck and fertility.

below SHIELD WITH HANDLE, *gaashaan.* Northern Somalia. Rhinoceros hide with geometrical repousse patterns. D. 35cm. 19th Century. Collection John and Elizabeth Johnson, Bloomington, Indiana.

opposite CAMEL WITH BELL. Caynabo. Photo Phoebe Ferguson, 1979.

COILED BASKET, *gorof.* Buloxaar. Fiber. H. 29cm, D. 29cm. Collection Abby Thomas, Washington, D.C. This basket is used to hold water, for milking camels, and as a drinking vessel.

opposite NOMAD holding his *gorof.* Photo Manfred Wehrmann.

When fortune places a man even on the mere hem of her robe
He quickly becomes proud and overbearing
A small milking vessell when filled to the brim soon overflows

Excerpt from a poem by Gabai Shinni

above GROUP OF NOMADS wearing amulets and holding headrests and canes. Middle Shabeelle. Photo Lee Cassanelli, 1977. Headrests are very common among nomads. Young men guarding animals at night use them so they do not sleep too soundly. It has also been said that they are used as protection against snakes and scorpions, and that nomadic men use them to protect their hair styles.

below HEADRESTS, *barkin*. Northern Somalia. Yucub wood. H. 20cm and 19cm respectively. Collection F.C.C.U., Washington, D.C.

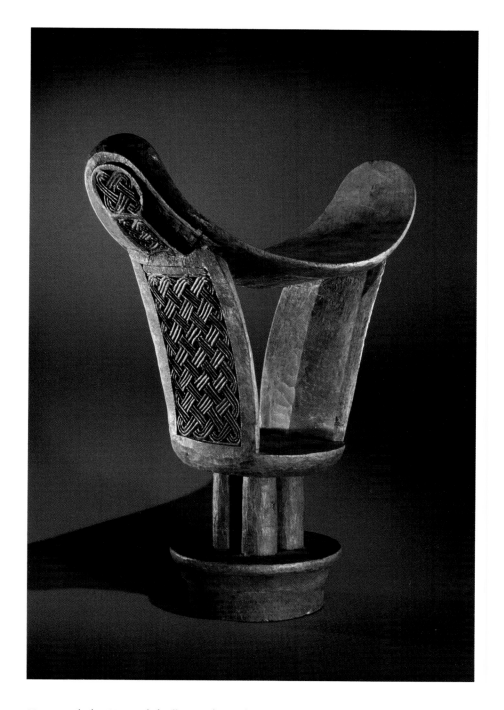

HEADREST, *barkin*. Upper Shabeelle. Yucub wood. H. 20cm. Collection Lee Cassanelli, Philadelphia, Pennsylvania. The headrest has a four pedestal column. It is carved with undulating plaited design.

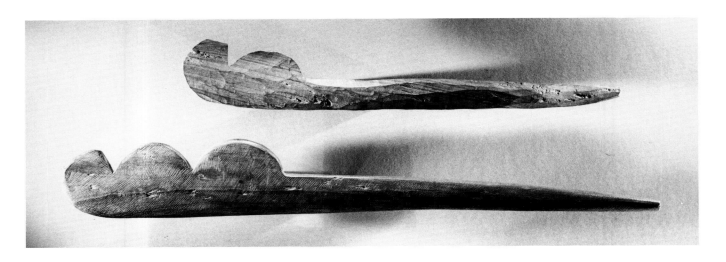

above AMULETS, *weger.* Sheekh. Carved wood. L. 45cm and 35cm respectively. Collection John and Elizabeth Johnson, Bloomington, Indiana. These amulets are used by women, who carry them in the hand as protection against the evil spirits, *shaydaan.*

below TWINED WEDDING BAG, *quandi.* Mogadishu. White, beige, black and red fibers. L. 85cm, W. 37cm. Collection Martin and Evelyn Ganzglass, Washington, D.C.

COILED BASKET, *haan.* Mogadishu. H. 42cm. Collection
Abby Thomas, Washington, D.C. This type of basket
is used throughout Somalia to carry food, such as dried
meats and clarified butter, and to carry milk.

WOMAN tying border of mat. Photo Manfred Wehrmann.

opposite TWINED MAT (detail), *caws.* Northern Somalia. Grass embellished with turquoise and violet yarns. L. 182cm, W. 77cm. Collection Somali National Museum, Mogadishu. Used as a wall covering inside the *aqal.* A mat is often named after the woman who designed and created it. When it is finished women friends are invited to help tie the fringe. They celebrate the mat's completion, singing and dancing the praises of the artist and her product.

O weaving reeds, may you never be poverty stricken
May you never be taken for sale in the market
May none be ignorant of your maker
May no unworthy man ever tread on you

Anonymous women's work song

When you are seeking peace, send for the old and the learned
but if they fail you the spear point becomes a necessity

Proverb

left SPEAR HEADS, *warran.* Northern Somalia. Iron with decorative geometrical incisions. L. 38½cm and 69cm respectively. Collection John and Elizabeth Johnson, Bloomington, Indiana.

right STICK WITH ROUNDED EYE, *budh.* Sheekh. Wood with geometrical incisions. L. 75cm. Collection John and Elizabeth Johnson, Bloomington, Indiana.

opposite NOMADS herding cattle, holding spears. Northern Somalia. Photo Phoebe Ferguson, 1979.

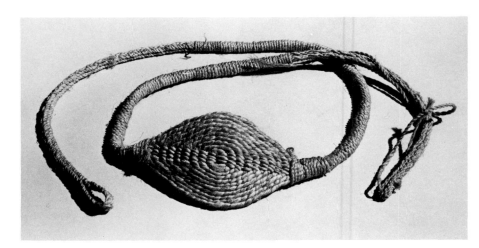

left STICK WITH HOOK AND FORK, *hangool*. Southern Somalia. Wood. L. 86cm. Collection John and Elizabeth Johnson, Bloomington, Indiana. Traditionally presented to a groom on his wedding day, this tool is used by nomadic men and is regarded as the symbol of the herdsman. The forked end is used to edge the thorn bushes out of the ground, and the hooked edge is used to drag the bush.

above right STRAP, *cayn*. Northern Somalia. Twined fiber, leather and cowrie shells. L. 300cm. Collection Somali National Museum, Mogadishu. This type of strap is used to secure loads on camels.

below right SLINGSHOT, *waraf* or *wadhaf*. Southern Somalia. Fiber. L. 155cm. Collection John and Elizabeth Johnson, Bloomington, Indiana. The small loop is secured on the index finger, a stone is placed in the pocket, the loose end is held in the hand. It is swung back and forth until enough momentum has been gained to raise it above the head. When aimed, one end of the rope is let go and the stone flies towards its target. Because of its speed, *waraf* is the word used in contemporary Somalia for airmail.

opposite NOMADS on trek with packed camels holding their *aqals*. Northern Somalia. Photo Phoebe Ferguson, 1979.

The camels are packed and ready for the weary trek
And men's thoughts dwell on distant destinations

Excerpt from a poem by Axmed Ismaaciil Diiriye

The home we have set up, the bed I had spread for you
The trust between us, our resolve and the oath
If you have turned away from all these and abandoned me in a deserted place
Then it was sheer folly that possessed me

Excerpt from a poem by Xasan Sheekh Muumin

above NOMADIC VILLAGE, *aqals* surrounded by thorn branch fences. Northern Somalia. Photo Phoebe Ferguson, 1979.

below PLAITED MAT *(detail), caws.* Northern Somalia. Grass. L. 190cm, W. 150cm. Collection Somali National Museum, Mogadishu. These mats are used as the outer and inner walls of the nomadic house, *aqal.*

opposite NOMADIC WOMAN AND CHILDREN. The woman is building an *aqal,* or nomadic house, in Northern Somalia. The armature of the house is made of curved and bound branches (seen here) and poles. Once the structure is completed, it is covered with skins and three layers of mats. The inner layer or inside wall is made of decorated mats. Traditionally, it is the woman's role to set up the *aqal.* Photo Manfred Wehrmann.

VUE DE GUÉLEDI
sur la rivière Dessej

above VIEW OF GELEDDI. From C. Guillain, *Voyage à la Côte Orientale d'Afrique,* Plate 26. E. Ciceri Lith., Vayot, and A. Bertrand, Editor, Paris, 1856. The town of Geleddi is now known as Afgooye. In the last century it was the seat of the Geleddi Sultanate, said to have been one of the most powerful in the region. Figure, courtesy Cambridge University Library.

below AFGOOYE in 1968. Photo Virginia Luling.

SOCIETY AND CULTURE IN THE RIVERINE REGION OF SOUTHERN SOMALIA

Lee V. Cassanelli

While Somalia is best known as a nation of nomadic pastoralists, not all of its people depend on livestock for their living. In fact, some 25 percent of the Somali population are full- or part-time farmers. Most of these farmers live either along the banks of the Jubba or Shabeelle rivers, where irrigation makes sedentary agricultural life possible, or in the interriver plains, where seasonal rainfall permits the local inhabitants to combine farming with livestock rearing. Agriculture in southern Somalia goes back almost two millennia, even though some of the present-day inhabitants of the region have taken up farming in relatively recent times. Evidence from archaeology and historical linguistics is beginning to accumulate to suggest that the ancestors of at least some of today's Somalis practiced a mixed economy of farming and herding in the interriver region well before other groups of Somali-speakers occupied the more arid zones of the northern and central Horn.

Unfortunately, the history and cultural traditions of the riverine regions[1] of Somalia are not nearly as well known to outsiders as those of the pastoral zones to the north and south. This relative neglect of riverine society stems in part from the particular fascination that the more strictly pastoral way of life holds for students of Somalia. It is also the case that, until recently, most research on southern Somalia was done by Italian scholars, whose publications were not widely read in the English-speaking world. Then, too, the development of a written Somali language, which is based on that dialect group spoken in the northern two-thirds of the country, has led scholars to focus on the literary and poetic traditions of the north, leaving the riverine region as a secondary field for the study of Somali language dialects and traditions.

As I hope to demonstrate, the riverine peoples of Somalia have a rich and diversified oral and material culture of their own, which, while it shares much with the pastoral tradition that has interpenetrated it for centuries, nonetheless reflects the particular environment and unique history of the region.

The first thing one notices about the riverine region is the great variety of social groups, language dialects, and economic activities found there. Ethnographers have long noted the diversity of communities and complexity of social organization in southern Somalia, in marked contrast to the more homogeneous pastoral culture that characterizes the rest of the Somali peninsula. Colucci,[2] Lewis,[3] and Luling,[4] have described how many of the so-called tribes of southern Somalia are in fact confederations of lineages and lineage segments of diverse genealogical and

67

geographical origins. As migrating families of nomads and seminomads moved historically into the riverine area in search of water and better pastures for their herds, they attached themselves as "clients," or dependents, to previously established settlers. If the newcomers remained for several generations, they gradually were incorporated into the political structure of the community and came to share fully in its resources. While the people still used a kinship idiom to describe the relationships among the various components of these southern confederations, what in fact held them together was residence in a common territory and loyalty to a common political or religious authority.

Even more striking than the mosaic of Somali lineage groups that were fused together over time to form the large territorial confederations was the region's capacity to assimilate peoples of non-Somali origins. Along the lower Shabeelle Valley, for instance, there resided groups of settlers known as Gibilcad (literally, "white skins"), who in the early twentieth century claimed Arab origins and were considered by their neighbors to have special religious powers.

While the "white skins" may indeed have descended from groups of religious refugees from Arabia or from transplanted Arab families originally resident in the Benaadir coastal towns, by the early twentieth century they all spoke Somali and participated as full members in the social and political life of the local Somali communities in whose territories they lived.[5]

In the upper Jubba River basin, Oromo (Galla) and Somali communities have intermingled and intermarried for centuries, with the result that some of the "Somali" confederations in that area contained lineages that were almost certainly Oromo in origin.[6] Many inhabitants of the Gedo region today are bilingual in Somali and Oromo.

Finally, captives from the Bantu-speaking regions of East Africa who were brought to southern Somalia as slaves during the brief period in the nineteenth century when plantation agriculture flourished along the Shabeelle River remained in the riverine area after slavery was abolished in 1904. While some fled to freed-slave villages along the Jubba River, others continued to work as free farmers on the irrigated lands along the Shabeelle. Early colonial authorities found it almost impossible to distinguish between these ex-slaves and the descendants of much older cultivating communities that had preceded them: both groups spoke Somali, farmed their own land, and intermarried. Even in recent times, local pastoral Somalis sometimes disdained the farmers because of their presumed non-Somali origins. But the very fact that the farmers today speak Somali and make up the backbone of the agricultural economy of the south attests to the strength of the assimilative tradition of the riverine region.

The diverse genealogical and geographic origins of the riverine region's inhabitants are mirrored in the complex linguistic structure of the area. Recent research has revealed that more than a dozen distinct Somali dialects are spoken along and between the rivers.[7]At least seven of these (some with subdialects) belong to the so-called Maay branch of the Somali language tree, and it is the Maay speakers who form the majority of semisedentary and settled cultivators of the riverine region. In addition, we find several dialects of the Maxaad or Northern branch of Somali spoken in the interriver area, and some of these speakers clearly represent groups of pastoralists who immigrated into the region in relatively recent times, over the past two or three centuries. Finally, the dialects known as Jiiduu, Garree, and Tunni are spoken by Somalis who occupy the southwestern quadrant of the interriver zone; these Somalis may represent the descendants of the earliest Somali-speakers to have settled in the country today known as Somalia. While much more linguistic research needs to be undertaken in the south, what is emerging is a picture of remarkable linguistic diversity that suggests a complex social and cultural history.

The economy of the riverine region is as varied as its inhabitants. Agriculture (both irrigated and rain-fed) and animal husbandry (of both cattle and camels) are practiced in varying combinations. The "red-earth" districts of the interriver plain are ideal for the grazing of camels; while the "black-earth" districts along the rivers and around the springs of Baydhabo support extensive cultivation of millet, maize, and vegetables. In the transitional zones between red and black districts, people practice a mixed economy of cattle raising and rain-fed farming. Towns such as Baydhabo, Dhiinsoor, Buur Hakaba, and Wanle Weyn also serve as market centers where pastoral and agricultural produce is exchanged, and where handicrafts such as mats, pots, woven containers, and headrests can be purchased.

The continuum of farming and herding lifestyles in southern Somalia is reflected in the proverbial wisdom of the region's traditional weather-lore experts. Combining their long experience in observing wind and rainfall patterns with a sizable knowledge of the stars and constellations, these experts attempt to forecast whether the year to come will bring prosperity or hard times. They speak of three kinds of years: *laba-mooyaale* ("two mortars"), *laba-maalisley* ("two milkings"), and *laba-maylinley* ("two spears"). A *laba-mooyaale* year is one in which rainfall is so abundant that "two mortars" will be needed to grind and process all the millet that will be harvested. A *laba-maalisley* year is one in which crops may fail, but the grazing will be plentiful enough to insure "two milkings" of the animals each day. However, a *laba-maylinley* year is one when both crops and grazing are in short supply: one spear represents the warfare and looting that follow upon such scarcity, the other the need to slaughter livestock and carry it to the cooking pot before drought and disease deplete the herds. In this traditional weather lore, then, we see how the riverine Somalis have integrated farming and herding to achieve the maximum yield which the land can provide.[8]

In all probability, the earliest inhabitants of the riverine region were neither farmers nor herders, but rather small groups of hunters. These in all likelihood were descendants of Later Stone Age populations, whose rock shelters and stone artifacts have been uncovered by archaeologists at Buur Hakaba, Buur Heybe, and elsewhere in the interriver region.[9] Small groups of hunters still roamed the more remote bush country of the Upper Jubba basin in the early twentieth century. They used bows and arrows tipped with a poisonous substance known as *wabayo,* which was derived from boiling the pulverized roots of the *acocathera wabayo poiss.* During the eighteenth and nineteenth centuries, and presumably in earlier times, the hunters provided the elephant ivory and rhinoceros horn that constituted two of the major exports of the interriver region. They also made durable shields of rhinoceros, giraffe, and oryx skins.[10]

Another early group of inhabitants was the riverine farmers of the middle and lower Shabeelle River valley. Some scholars believe that these early farmers were part of a large-scale population movement that brought Bantu-speaking cultivators to many parts of eastern Africa in the first half of the first millennium A.D.[11] If these settled farmers once spoke Bantu languages, however, they long since have been assimilated linguistically by the Somalis. What confuses the historical picture even more is the existence of contemporary communities of Bantu-speaking farmers along the lower Jubba River.[12] These are almost certainly the descendants of escaped slaves who sought refuge from their former masters in the densely wooded lands along the Jubba in the later nineteenth century.[13] As we have seen, it is almost impossible today to distinguish physically between riverine farmers who may have an ancient history in the area and those of more recent venue in Somalia. As we shall see below, both groups have contributed substantially to the material culture of the riverine region.

The Somalis' occupation of the Horn of Africa has been the subject of considerable debate among scholars. Some contend that the Somalis began their expansion from a point along the shores of the Gulf of Aden, while others argue that they began from the region between the head-waters of the Jubba River and Lake Turkana, in what is today northern Kenya.[14] Linguistic evidence strongly supports the second hypothesis, for reconstructed proto-Somali seems to share many features with Ren-dille and Bayso, languages spoken today in northern Kenya and southern Ethiopia. The great diversity of dialects found in the interriver region also suggests that this area was an early and important dispersal point for subsequent Somali migrations.

It now seems increasingly probable that the ancestors of the earliest Somali speakers were raising camels on the plains of northern Kenya in the late first millennium B.C.; that some diversification of dialect communities had already begun by that time; and that several groups of southern Somali speakers had occupied portions of the interriver area by the early first millennium A.D., if not earlier. Toward the end of this latter period, it may be that groups of pastoralists pushed farther north into the pastures of central and northern Somalia, which may have been wetter in the first millenium A.D. than they are today. These northern groups adapted to their new environment through the very specialized form of nomadic pastoralism that we associate with the Somalis today.

Much of the foregoing historical reconstruction is necessarily still very speculative. However, historical and oral traditional evidence makes it clear that in more recent times (perhaps beginning as early as 1100 A.D.), the pattern of Somali population movement began to reverse itself. Nomadic families and lineage groups began to migrate from the more arid regions of the north toward the better-watered plains of the inter-river region. Their movements may have been prompted by population growth, excessive or prolonged periods of drought, or warfare associated with the spread of Islam and its frequent clashes with the Christian emperors of Ethiopia in the western Ogaadeen between the thirteenth and the sixteenth centuries.

One of the most famous groups to occupy the riverine region during this second phase of Somali migration history was the legendary Ajuraan. This powerful confederation of pastoral clans dominated the lower and middle Shabeelle Valley from the fifteenth through the seventeenth centuries. Oral traditions throughout the riverine area still recall their military might and oppressive rule; they seized the most important wells in the area and are said to have used slaves to construct canals for irrigation along the Shabeelle. The many ruined stone buildings that still dot the southern Somali countryside are said by local historians to have been fortifications built by Ajuraan rulers.[15]

In addition to collecting tribute from farmers and nomads in the region, the Ajuraan rulers appear to have made an alliance with the Muzaffar, a family prominent in the politics of the coastal town of Muqdisho. This alliance helped promote trade between the riverine region controlled by the Ajuraan and the markets of the Benaadir coast. It was during these years that the economy of the riverine region was integrated firmly into the trade of the western Indian Ocean.

Eventually, the inhabitants of the region rebelled against Ajuraan rule and, according to tradition, drove them out of the country after a long series of battles. A series of smaller polities then arose in the region, the most powerful of which was the Geledi sultanate centered in the Shabeelle River town of Afgooye. By the 1850s, the sultan of Geledi headed an alliance of clans that extended north to Baydhabo and southeast along the coast to Baraawe. His power rested in a combination of religious prestige and the wealth he extracted from the farm lands along the Shabeelle and from caravan traders whose route to Muqdisho crossed the river at Afgooye. Geledi's preeminence in the riverine area did not go unchallenged. Its sultans fought several battles with the Biyamaal warriors in the hinterland of Marka. And in 1843, forces loyal to the Geledi sultan waged a momentous battle against an army of religious reformers based in the Jubba River town of Baardheere. The battle, which grew out of disputes over religious and political authority in the region, as well as over competition for control of the long-distance ivory trade, resulted in a Geledi victory and firmly established the Geledi sultan as the supreme power in the riverine region. The townspeople of Muqdisho consulted him on crucial political matters, and the sultans of Zanzibar even sent gifts and letters to him in recognition of his importance in the economic and political affairs of the region.[16]

This very cursory history of the riverine region reveals its importance as the area where the pastoral, agricultural, and coastal traditions met. The relative abundance of water and pasture in the region meant that it served as a refuge zone for migrating pastoralists over much of the past millennium. The resources of the area made it attractive to ambitious rulers, and its grain helped feed the coastal towns of Muqdisho, Marka, and Baraawe from their beginnings in the first millennium A.D. The ivory and aromatic woods which crossed the region in caravans from the distant interior served to link the riverine peoples with the larger trading world of the Indian Ocean coast.

The rich history of riverine Somalia and the interaction of the many traditions that met there are quite naturally reflected in the region's material culture. The variety of simple but efficient agricultural implements—hoes, digging sticks, and plow boards—along with farming know-how represents the most enduring contribution of the Negroid cultivating populations. While most of the terminology today used in measuring, planting, and harvesting fields uses Somali words—as do the farmers themselves—some hint of agriculture's probable Bantu origins in Somalia comes from the most common words for hoe *(yaambo)* and scraping board *(kewawa).*

The distinctive houses *(mundul)* of the sedentary cultivators are today, as they were in the past, round mud-and-wattle structures erected around a central wooden pillar, with roof beams that support thatched roofs. Wealthier farmers frequently employ carpenters to provide them with finely carved wooden doors that reflect the influence of the Swahili-Arab carvings of the coast. Whenever houses had to be rebuilt or replaced, the center post, beams, doors, and lintels were saved, since the large trees from which they were cut were rare even along the Shabeelle. Woodwork was maintained and protected from the ubiquitous termite by staining it with a preparation called *assab,* which is obtained by boiling a reddish wood of the same name and which gives the wood its distinctive shiny dark surface.[17] Most woodworking is done by the cultivating population: in addition to wooden dishes, ladles and spoons, mortars and pestles, and hoe and axe handles, they also produce the finely carved headrests used by the distinctly coiffured Garre pastoralists of the region.

Together with the artisans of the coastal towns, the settled farmers did most of the local weaving, as well. Women spun cotton yarn imported from the coast into cloth of considerable durability. While most rural Somalis wore plain-colored garments, wealthier individuals often added a border of silk or gauze imported from India.

One of the more interesting groups of riverine society was the *baxaar,* or "fisher-ferrymen." Formerly held to be of low social status, they nonetheless performed the critical task of carrying livestock and people across the Shabeelle River in flat-bottomed rafts made of planks held together with heavy rope. The *baxaar* were reputed to have special powers that enabled them to summon and command the river crocodiles that were greatly feared by the farmers of the region. The *baxaar* provide a good illustration of how riverine society depended for much of its material and spiritual well-being on the services of the so-called low-status groups. Farmers, carpenters, weavers, and fisher-ferrymen not only provided the basis for the relative economic prosperity of riverine society through much of its history; they also contributed to the region's distinctive cultural profile and to its well-deserved reputation for hospitality.

While settled village life characterizes much of riverine Somalia, the vast plains of the interriver area are also home to large numbers of transhumant pastoralists. During the two annual rainy seasons, camels and cattle are kept at a healthy distance from the riverbanks, where the tse-tse fly breeds. But during the dry seasons, the animals are brought to water at the river's edge and occasionally to graze on the stubble of cut maize and millet. In exchange, local farmers receive fresh supplies of meat and milk from the herdsmen.

In the past, it was common for pastoral clans to form alliances with particular agricultural communities, to whom they provided protection in exchange for access to water and grain. Nowadays, many southern Somalis have investments in both farming and livestock. Which type of existence is most desirable has always been the subject of debate among Somalis of the region. There is a story told of a nomadic poet who once tried his hand at farming in the belief that it would offer him contentment and an easier life. In the end, he rejected the settled life and explained his decision in the following *gabay:*[18]

> It is said that one cannot pierce the sky to get rain
>   for one's garden,
> Nor can one drive the farm, as one drives animals, to
>   the place where the rain is falling
> Worst of all, one cannot abandon one's farm, even though
>   barren, because all one's efforts are invested in it.

The farmer, of course, has his own argument to counter with:

> A man with no fixed place in this world cannot claim
>   one in heaven.

Before concluding this brief essay on the riverine communities of Somalia, something must be said about the influence of Islam on the area. Virtually all riverine people, whatever their origins and cultural backgrounds, claim today to be Muslims. While many of the region's annual communal festivals—such as the *dabshid,* or "fire-lighting" cere-mony, to begin the solar new year, or the famous *istun* ("stick fight") of Afgooy town—may have pre-Islamic or nonreligious origins, Islamic ritual pervades the public life of riverine society. Every village has its small mosque, and the countryside is dotted with the whitewashed tombs of long-deceased saints, whose lives fill a substantial part of the region's oral traditions.

These traditions make it clear that Islam penetrated southern Somalia not in the form of a militant conquest but in a centuries-long process of conversion through the efforts of countless itinerant holy men. Many of these preachers and teachers studied in the Benaadir coastal towns and later carried the teachings of the Prophet to the settlements and watering sites of the interior. The Muslim holy men also contributed to riverine society in another way: they helped to settle disputes and intro-duce a common legal tradition. For in a region of such social and ethnic diversity, the role of peacemaker and mediator was a critical one. This role was filled largely by the saints, and there are many stories in the oral tradition that attest to their centrality in building the multiclan communities characteristic of riverine Somalia.

One such tradition, which I recorded in an interview with a prominent elder in 1977, describes the work of a holy man known as Omar "Arag" (literally, Omar "the Seer"), who lived two to three hundred years ago:

> Omar "Arag" helped to organize the Rahanwiin tribes around Sara-man. At that time, the people were divided into two sections and were always fighting with the Arussi and Borana [Oromo]. Omar appointed *malaakhs* to lead the army, organized trade among the tribes, and set boundaries for each.
>
> He was the first person to divide the 114 suras of the Quran among the various local clans. Even today, the various clans come together at his tomb [in Saraman] every year. Each brings with them a *loox* [piece of wood on which Quranic verses are written]. Then one of the descendants of Omar "Arag" washes the verses off the *loox* and the water which runs off is divided among the various clans to protect them.

In this tradition and countless others, we see how contemporary rituals draw on oral tradition to help recreate and reinforce the community solidarity that is essential in a region where diversity is the rule rather than the exception. In the oral traditions and ritual celebrations of the riverine region, as in its material culture, we see evidence of both the diversity and the tradition of incorporation that constitute its special heritage for Somalia.

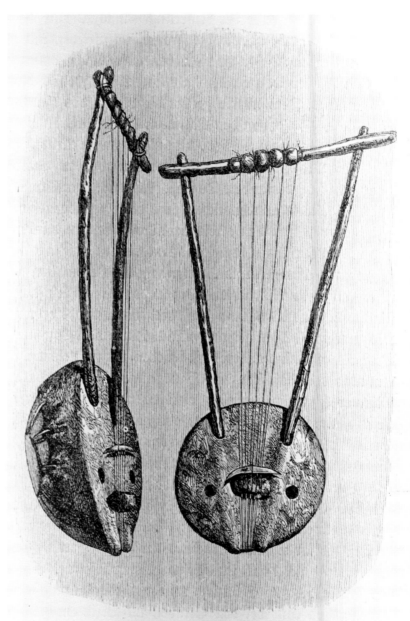

MUSICAL INSTRUMENT. From F. Ratzel, *Völkerkunde,* p. 433. Zweiter Band, Bibliographisches Institut, Leipzig und Wien, 1895.

Nubische Rabbaba. (Hagenbecks Sammlung, Hamburg.)
¹/₈ wirkl. Größe.

FLAT BOTTOMED RIVER RAFT used to cross the Shabeelle river. Outskirts of Afgooye. Photo Virginia Luling, 1968.

opposite MAN plowing with oxen. Photo Phoebe Ferguson, 1979.

A man with no land on earth will have no land in heaven
Proverb

YOUNG WOMAN wearing a leather cape decorated with cowrie shells. Afgooye. Photograph Virginia Luling, 1968.

Market place in Afgooye. Photo Virginia Luling, 1968.

above WOODEN DOOR heavily studded with metal (detail). Afgooye. Photo Virginia Luling, 1968.

below DECORATIVE ROUNDEL. Southern Somalia. Carved wood in the Azanian style. D. 55cm. Collection Giovanni Ferrero, Rome. This roundel is from the apex of a house, and typical of those found in Southern Somalia.

ENTRANCE TO A HOUSE in Afgooye. Photo Virginia Luling, 1968.

Child weaving basket near Afgooye. Photo Manfred Wehrmann.

TWINED MILK CONTAINER WITH LID, *dheel*. Afgooye. Fiber, leather and cowrie shells. H. 26½cm, D. 10½cm. Collection F.C.C.U., Washington., D.C.

above PEDESTAL BOWL WITH HANDLE, *kurbun.* Afgooye. Wood. L. 38½cm, D. 21cm. Collection Virginia Luling, London. This type of bowl is used to serve roasted coffee beans.

below LADLE or water scoop, *kalax.* Jennali. Wood, carved from a single piece. L. 44cm. Private Collection.

CONTAINER WITH LID, *dheel*. Upper Jubba. Wood and leather. H. 31cm. Collection Lee Cassanelli, Philadelphia, Pennsylvania. This type of container is used to store milk.

CERAMIC POT. Mogadishu. Clay. H. 14cm, D. 19cm. Collection F.C.C.U., Washington, D.C.

opposite WOMAN SPLATTERING POTS for decoration. Outskirts of Mogadishu. Photo Manfred Wehrmann.

POTTERS firing pots, outskirts of Mogadishu. Photo Manfred Wehrmann.

opposite WOMEN drawing water, north of Marka. Photo Phoebe Ferguson, 1979.

Wherever one looks, the life of this world depends on water
But if the water itself feels thirsty,
From what well can one quench its thirst?

Excerpt from a poem by Xasan Sheekh Muumin

DRUM, *durbaan.* Mogadishu. Wood and goatskin. H. 65cm, D. 22cm. Collection Somali National Museum, Mogadishu. This drum is made of a hollowed tree trunk.

above DANCERS, Mogadishu. Photo, photographic Officer, USS. Vreeland, 1978.

below MUSICAL INSTRUMENT, *shareero*. Mogadishu. Wood, hide and string. L. 75cm. Private Collection.

I bade you farewell. Wished you a journey full of blessing;
Every hour you exist, when you go to sleep and when you awake
Keep in mind the troth between us
I am waiting for you, come safely back, come safely back

Excerpt from a poem by Maxamuud Tukaale

Road near Jennali. Photo Phoebe Ferguson, 1979.

opposite Young woman near Jennali. Photo Phoebe Ferguson, 1979.

FISHERMEN on the Shabeelle River. Photo Manfred Wehrmann.

opposite FISHERMAN on the Shabeelle River. Photo Manfred Wehrmann.

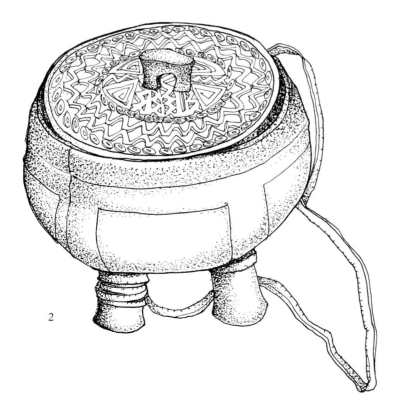

2

SOMALI WOOD ENGRAVINGS

Vinigi L. Grottanelli

No person interested in African art can have failed to be struck by a conspicuous feature related to the geographical distribution of its creative centers. In sharp contrast to the name-studded areas in the west and center of the continent, all maps accompanying the countless surveys of these arts, whether treatises or exhibition catalogues, show a regular blank surface covering the eastern regions. That has resulted in conveying the somewhat stereotyped, though not altogether untruthful, image of a sub-Saharan Africa split in two by a chasm running from north to south roughly along the Rift Valley depression. All the artistically fertile peoples would be clustered west of this imaginary line, and all the artistically sterile ones conveniently grouped east of it, the Makonde group constituting an unaccountable and unruly exception.

Placed at the extreme northeastern limits of the sterile half, the Somali occupy a special position. Racially, linguistically, and culturally, they have little or nothing in common with the Negro world, to which we owe the manifold styles of African sculpture. The traditional economy of all their tribes, from the Gulf of Aden to the Equator and beyond, is based on pastoralism. In Africa as elsewhere, nomadism has notoriously engendered a detached attitude, if not an outright contempt, toward the material possessions and handicrafts of the sedentary peoples. There is something noble and almost ascetic in the obstinacy displayed by this proud and handsome nation of herdsmen in remaining faithful to a Biblical pattern of life, spurning all but the barely essential goods of the world, elated with the supreme freedom of a roaming existence that knows no boundaries under the open sky. Furthermore, the Somali are Moslems of long standing; as such, they reject and condemn all attempts to reproduce the living forms of man and animal—a severe limitation on artistic output. Little surprise, then, if their name is regularly absent from lists of art-producing African peoples.

Nevertheless, having twice visited their country, and having been for a quarter of a century the curator of an ethnographic museum possessing what is certainly one of the richest, if not the world's most complete, collection of Somali objects, I have always been aware that the Somali were, and are, far from indifferent to formal beauty. In the field of visual arts, their principal means of expression is wood engraving applied to the production and decoration of a limited series of everyday objects—such as can be expected of a hitherto entirely rural society fettered both by extreme poverty of technical equipment, and by the rules of an-iconic representation. Yet even the few artifacts published here will, I trust, con-

1. *Imbolo* pattern, Bushongo (Bakuba) of the Kasai.
2. Somali butter container. Acquired before 1898.

tribute to modify the negative judgment usually accepted by critics.

The carved window frame (Illus. 11), donated to the Rome museum in the early 1930s, comes from a building described as "an old Arab house in Mogadiscio." As regards the age of the object, though the house may well have been ancient, examination of the wood shows that the frame itself is relatively recent, probably not earlier than 1890 or 1900. The reference to an "Arab" house by no means implies that the craftsman must also have been an Arab; in fact, I consider it a typical product of local (coastal) craftmanship.

Mogadiscio, as is well known, was founded by Arabian and possibly also Persian immigrants early in the tenth century A.D. and remained mainly an Arab colony and a trade center for over 300 years. But the nomadic Somali tribes who controlled the hinterland, and in course of time surrounded the city, no doubt began to infiltrate at an early date; around 1250 A.D., Mogadiscio already appears to be a mixed Arabo-Somali sultanate; and in 1573 a document lists the town's tribes with Somali names, no longer the Arab ones.[1] The town's architecture, and its culture in general, were originally of Arabian inspiration; but as centuries passed, a mixed culture arose here, as well as in similar coastal centers farther south, from Merca, Brava, Lamu, and Malindi, to Mombasa and Zanzibar, to Kilwa Kisiwani in present-day Tanzania, and down to Sofala in Mozambique. Immigrants from various regions of the Arabian peninsula, from the Persian Gulf coasts and southern Iran, from western India, and to a lesser degree from Indonesia and even China, contributed to the formation of this widespread coastal culture, which can correctly be termed "Azanian," from the old Greek name of the East-African littoral. But Africans themselves, of both Cushitic and Bantu stock, participated in this formation, interbred to a certain extent with the Asiatic colonists and settlers, and assimilated their customs, including their standards of art and taste.

Unfortunately, we still lack a comprehensive study of the ornamental patterns typical of Azanian art, an excellent introduction to which has recently been given by J. Kirkman.[2] It is clear, however, that the two main elements in the incised decoration of window (11)—the twelve-petal rosette and the related four-petal "aster" encased in a quadrangular frame—belong to the classical style of the coastal towns and monuments. They are associated, for instance, on the lintel of the old "Persian monastery" at Lamu.[3] The latter motif appears in the plaster-and-gypsum decorative moldings on the walls of the Kunduchi buildings in southern Tanzania, which—I assume—belong to the later, eighteenth-century period of this site.[4] These and other Azanian motifs are part of an old artistic tradition, the persistence of which through the centuries is a significant feature of East African coastal art; indeed, they can be traced back to pre-Islamic Arabia. The four-petal aster pattern, along with the other simple motifs (concentric circles, series of slightly undulated oblique lines), is found engraved on a marble column base, probably from Shi-

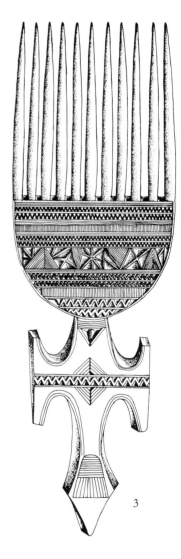

3. Somali comb. Collected before 1898 among the Gasar Gudda tribe of the Lugh region on the Jubba.
4. Incised comb with two separate rows of teeth. Bimal Somali near Merca.
5. Incised comb with two separate rows of teeth. Zanzibar.

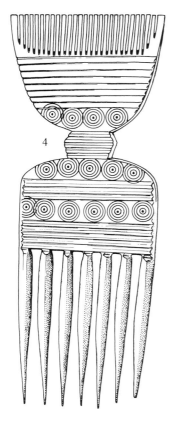

4

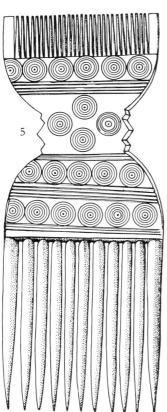

5

bām Kawkabān in Hadramawt, now in the Sana'ā museum; and the same type of rosette can be seen on the lintel of one of the famous Hegrā mausoleums dating back to the first century A.D.[5]

Another object revealing by its very nature an Asiatic "literate" origin is the Somali wooden inkstand, called *duad* (9). The ornamental pattern incised on the lid is too simple to permit specific, i.e., significant, comparisons. The undulating-ribbon motif, for instance, reminds the ethnologist of almost identical decorations in Massim engravings (S.E. New Guinea), but of course the parallel is purely incidental.

In contrast with these first two objects, obviously inspired by an "urban" type of culture, the wooden vase with engraved lid (2) is a traditional, plainly "rural" implement and leaves few doubts as to its having been produced by a Somali craftsman in the strict ethnic meaning of the adjective.[6] It is used for holding butter or curds. I think its artistic merits lie as much in its gracefully rounded shape, carved (with its four feet) out of a single block of soft wood, as in the elaborate lacelike design of the lid. Unfortunately, lack of catalogue data does not allow us to establish its exact tribal provenance.

Wooden combs are common among Cushitic as well as Swahili and other Bantu peoples of East Africa, although because of markedly different hair lengths they are functionally useful among the former, less so among the Swahili, and least among the relatively "pure" Negro peoples of the interior. It is obvious that apart from their practical utility, they are sought as fashionable items of elegance. All the specimens shown here belong to types that, according to most sources, are used by women, although no doubt Puccioni is right in saying that they are used by males —presumably young dandies—among those Somali tribes in which men also allow their hair to grow long.[7] These types are the most interesting ones for our present purpose, because of their larger size and flat surfaces which call for embellishment in the form of engraving. Older men sometimes have combs of much smaller size, usually not decorated at all, used for combing their beards, and hung (often along with iron pincers to extract thorns from their feet or pluck odd hair from eyebrows or chin) from the wooden grain necklaces described as "Muslim rosaries." They might also have hairpins with one, two, or even three prongs, cylindrical or flattened in form, which are sometimes minutely ornamented. A special type, to be worn by warriors who can boast the killing of an enemy, has a hole bored into the summit, into which an ostrich feather is inserted.[8]

The two combs with double rows of teeth provide as good a document of cultural borrowing as any diffusionist could desire. Specimen (5) comes from the Bimal Somali of the Merca region (1908), whereas (4) was collected in Zanzibar some thirty years earlier. The similarity in size, form, color of wood (almost black), and decoration is so striking that it cannot be fortuitous. The explanation is either that a Zanzibar model was introduced and then faithfully copied in coastal Somalia, or that the Zanzibar specimen belonged to Somali emigrants to that island. As matters of feminine combs were apparently judged trivial by travelers and scholars, I cannot find in the literature detailed descriptions or illustrations to support either alternative; but as Stuhlmann mentions that a type with a double row of teeth was used by Negro women in what is now coastal Tanzania, and with the knowledge that this type is rare among the Somali, the first alternative is the more likely.[9] It cannot even be excluded, in fact, that specimen (5) was merely an imported item among the Bimal.

6

The large type with a single row of teeth, predominant in Somalia, includes the most elaborately carved specimens known (3). There seem to be two fundamental types, according to the shape of the handle. The first type, which judging by its geographical distribution and its predominance among the northern Somali tribes I suggest has the best claims of being the "traditional" one, has a roughly triangular handle with an acute vertex, often ending with a lozenge-shaped knob at the top.[10] The second type has a more elaborately carved handle, with a symmetrical double-projecting crescent at the sides, or variants of this pattern, and is doubtless related to the Swahili type called *shanuo*, illustrated by Stuhlmann.[11] But both main types have given rise to so many varieties and intermediate subtypes that it is now difficult to draw a sharp dividing line between them. The implement is called *sakaf* in Ogaden and the north generally, *shirif* in Lugh and Bardera, and *shanle* in Merca and the neighboring zone of the southern coast.[12] The name *shanle* is related to swahili *shanuo,* and attention should be called to the fact that the same type of comb in Lugh, according to Ferrandi, is called *tana.* That is the Swahili verbal form "to comb," used as a noun in the diminutive form *kitana*, "small comb."[13] I am mentioning these linguistic details not out of idle curiosity but as further evidence that Swahili influences (and surely also artifacts) reached far inland into southern Somalia.

In the finest specimens, such as the one shown in (3), the formal grace and balance of the general outline, no doubt inspired by that of Somali *bilaw* dagger handles with their elegant ivory or horn-and-silver apexes, is matched by the beauty of the incised decoration, in which the unknown artist has played freely with geometrical patterns, ignoring the banal rules of symmetry.

The most perfect examples of Somali wood carving, however, are to be found among the spoons (7-10), called *fandar* or *fandal*. We are not concerned here with their functional uses, but the opinion put forward by Mochi, that these spoons were "more luxury objects and works of art than real utensils," is worth considering. If it is true, it could provide us with an example of a class of useless implements, produced as a mere pretext for artistic expression—evidence of an *art pour l'art* attitude, the very existence of which has been so strenuously denied at the level of nonliterate cultures.[14]

Factual data, however, do not entirely support this hypothesis in our

7

case. Whether used for stirring or sorting out such delicacies as coffee beans fried in butter, for preparing or dishing out their usual gruels, or for bringing these or other foods to the mouth, spoons and ladles are common in all parts of the Somali territory and show varying degrees of sophistication in their decoration—from the coarser ones with no incisions whatsoever, to the richly ornamented ones. The latter are also the smallest in size, but there is no indication that they, too, did not have a practical function—in this case possibly connected with the preparation and consumption of choice foods such as fried coffee beans, or for the entertainment of distinguished guests. The literature does not assist us in solving the problem, and archive materials in my museum are equally silent. Although one or more specimens of this type were ceded to the museum on eleven different occasions between 1881 and 1910, mostly by travelers and officials who had collected them personally, no mention of a special use is to be found in the accompanying lists and reports. All donors took it for granted that a wooden spoon was just a wooden spoon, requiring no further commentary.

We are better informed with regard to the provenance of the implements. Judging by our museum collections, the finest specimens come from the regions between Berbera and the upper Webi, i.e., from the northern tribes, and from the Mahaddei Wèn area on the middle course of the Webi.[15] The average quality of design and craftsmanship appears to be somewhat lower among the Jubaland Somali of Bardera and Lugh. The coarsest implements are those from the southern coastal areas of Merca and Brava. That is quite the contrary of what one would expect from the plausible assumption that the fashion of decorating spoons, like that of decorating implements, spread from the ancient Asian-colonized coastal cities on the Indian Ocean to the wild barren steppes of the interior. It could be argued, of course, that the sampling—based on eighty-odd specimens all told—need not necessarily be representative of the actual distribution, especially in an open country in which diffusion is facilitated by nomadism and has no doubt been operative for many a century. But comparison with objects of the same class in neighboring areas seems to confirm that distribution in that way is not altogether improbable or misleading.

Both from museum collections and from the literature, we know that decorated spoons of the same type are used north of the Somali, by the Galla of Harar, and in Shoa.[16] Indeed, the Bern museum series, illustrated by Rohrer and simply labeled "Abessinien," suggests such close parallels with the Somali types, in the unmistakable elongated shape of the bowl, as well as in the patterns incised on the handles (bands or triangles filled with oblique incised lines in alternate directions, chevrons, pearl motifs, minute cross-hatchings, etc.), that one regrets the lack of more precise provenance data.[17] The Zanzibar types known to me, on the other hand, show considerable differences from Somali ones, in both general form and decorative detail. One type is shown in (8).

8

6. Variation of an Azanian decorative pattern from the frieze of a Shirazi tombstone in coastal Tanzania. Before 1897.
7. Somali spoon. Collected in 1892 in the region between Berbera and the upper Webi.
8. Somali spoon. Obtained in 1898.

The fact that formal affinities, in this particular case, point more to the northwest (Ethiopia) than to the Swahili-influenced south does not authorize the hasty conclusion that this class of implements is beyond the range of Asiatic influences. Spoons—like combs—are of such universal use in East Africa, as elsewhere, and present such a variety of types and subtypes, that nothing short of a thorough analysis of all these could serve as a preamble to satisfactory comparisons and permit the drawing of some valid inferences. A preparatory study of this nature, far beyond the scope of this or any other single paper, has, to my knowledge, never been attempted. Indeed, one wonders whether it ever could be completed. Old types (significant clues in the study of a diffusion process) may well have been abandoned and superseded by new ones, both among African tribes and in the Asiatic countries which we know to have influenced East Africa, without leaving traces either in the areas concerned or in ethnographic and archaeological museums.

Single ornamental motifs, not tied to any particular class of objects, would also no doubt have an interesting story to tell, if they ever had been studied systematically in their geographical distribution. True, some of the simplest ones (e.g., chevrons, cross-hatchings, dot-and-circle) may have had multiple, unrelated origins in various places; but others are fair documents of cultural diffusion. As usual, a neat dividing line between the two categories is hard to draw. For instance, the undulated-plait pattern as seen on the handle of (7) has an understandably wide distribution in space and time, from the friezes of Carchemish eighth-century B.C. reliefs to modern Kalanga (Mashonaland) knife sheaths and Merina (Madagascar) bed boards, from Benin seventeenth-century ivories to contemporary Yoruba divination trays. Applied to a cylindrical surface, as in (8), the plait motif acquires a different aspect, which finds parallels in Zulu engraved spoons—possibly a convergence accounted for by elementary technical reasons.[18] But when the simple plait motif develops into a double-interlocking elliptical loop, as in the handle of the left-hand spoon of (10), the parallel with the corresponding Azanian motif—used, for instance, in a Shirazi tombstone frieze (6) dated 1660, published by von Luschan—can hardly be dismissed as purely casual, historical connections of the Somali with Azanian centers being an established historical reality.[19] Indeed, although similar contacts between the latter and the central Congo are far from being proved, one may doubt whether the identical Bushongo pattern called *imbolo*, used in embroidery, wood carving, and wall decoration (1), has had an independent origin.[20]

At any rate, individual ornamental motifs—whether or not of heterogeneous provenance—are elements that acquire their artistic significance only when integrated into a whole. Even if we accept Paulitschke's statement that Somali and Galla decorative patterns are derived from Arab models, that does not detract from our appreciation of the spoons and other incised implements, as an original creation of Somali inven-

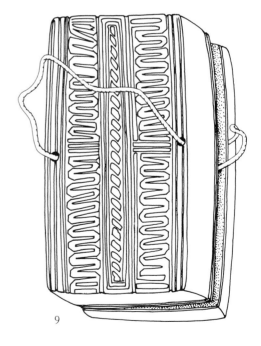

9

9. Somali ink stand from the Bimal of Merca. Collected in 1908.

tiveness and taste.[21] In the case of the spoons, even the general form does not appear to be copied from Azanian models, but rather from original Cushitic prototypes; and whether the decoration may have been partly inspired by old Arab influences from the Red Sea and Aden Gulf areas, and not wholly by the more southern centers on the Indian Ocean, is difficult to assess, considering the ancient influences from both directions on the peoples of the African Horn.

And lastly, of course, the question arises: who were, and are, the anonymous artisans who actually produced the engraved wooden objects? The technical ability displayed in most of these works leaves no doubt as to the fact that their authors were skilled craftsmen, with "specialized" experience in this kind of workmanship. But did such men emerge because of personal talent and inclination from among the "noble" tribal herdsmen, or did they belong to one or another of the so-called low castes, or to the Bantu minorities?[22] Were the spoons, combs, etc. made by the very groups who used them throughout the country, or by specialized craftsmen concentrated in a few localities, and then traded far and wide as imported commodites?

Though the objects themselves have often been described, collected, and reproduced in books, these simple questions appear to have received little or no attention. Referring to the northern Somali, Paulitschke says that wood engravings (he specifically mentions spoons and bowls) "are produced in the coastal sites only in small quantities"; but in his later work he writes, "The ability to carve wood is very widespread and young people often occupy thus their time while they are pasturing their herds."[23] Stuhlmann's remarks are pertinent to our subject, though they concern the southern neighbors of the Somali, not the Somali themselves. He speaks of "special craftsmen" producing the women's combs (similar to those in Illus. 3), and adds:

> These intaglio works are the only ornament known to the coastal Negro; he uses them to decorate spoon handles, etc. Where the pattern originally comes from is uncertain. Its use on old graves however makes me surmise that it is of Persian-Arab origin; in the interior it is unknown....These spoons are altogether produced as foreign craftsmanship, just like the combs....There are not many Negroes who are carpenters or joiners (sermadda), this kind of handicraft does not suit them much. In the field of domestic industries they do produce their mortars, drums, combs, spoons, and indeed also bed stands and caskets... but in general for finer works one always takes Indian joiners, Hindus (Banyans) much more often than Moslems.[24]

The typewritten catalogue by an unknown Italian official, describing a large Bimal ethnographic collection (Merca region in southern Somalia), now owned by the Rome museum, mentions the fact that woodworkers, as well as smiths, in that area are of Swahili origin, but born in Somalia; in the interior, it adds, these crafts are carried on by liberated slaves (also of Negro origin). Puccioni doubtfully suggests that the Somali may have acquired the craft of wood carving from the Negroid

10. Somali spoons. Collected in 1881.

peoples inhabiting the banks of the two major rivers (the Webi and the Juba).[25] Lewis, following Puccioni, writes, "Wooden *objets d'art* are distributed sparsely but extensively and the main centers of production are in the south, at Hakaba, on the Juba, Bender Kassim, Baidoa, Jelib, and Uddur—the best known center in the south where trade is mainly for the external Western market."[26]

That the Somali, like the Swahili and the eastern Bantu in general, were judged to be mediocre craftsmen in woodwork, according to European standards, or even to the Asiatic standards Stuhlmann had in mind, is of course beside the point; that they were basically not interested in sculpture of any kind, and that—again like the Swahili—they are indebted to the leaven of Asiatic colonization for the types and patterns of their decorative art, is a highly probable and, in some cases, a proven fact. Yet, they not only proved receptive to foreign stimuli but integrated them into fairly original forms, revealing ingenuity in execution and unfailing good taste in their simplicity. None of the objects I have briefly illustrated is a passive copy of an alien model, and the same can be said of other classes of similarly engraved wooden implements I have not discussed, such as headrests, bowls and plates, drinking beakers, water bottles, spear supports, drums, mortars, flat triangular wedges inserted in hut walls and used as hangers, ceiling-top discs, and small boxes.

Despite lacunae in our knowledge about the early trends and formative periods of this production, one cannot doubt that at least by the nineteenth century it was part of a well-established cultural tradition in most parts of the immense Somali territory—a tradition that was Cushitic as well as Azanian in its developments, and that had acquired, in its own right, full African citizenship. It is to be feared that here, as elsewhere, the impact of modern civilization will prove detrimental, if not fatal, to the survival of these delicate forms of craftsmanship, and that soon the finest objects will be seen only in museums.[27] But as it is, I feel that Somali wood engraving deserves to be saved from oblivion, more keenly studied and appreciated, and recognized as ranking not least among traditional African art styles.

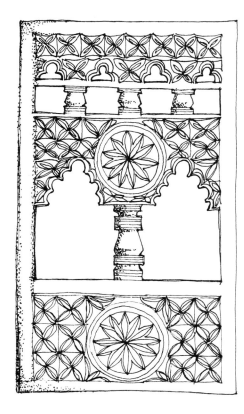

11

11. Carved window from "an old Arab house in Mogadiscio," 1890 or 1900.

MOGADISHU. From E. Cerulli, *Somalia, Scritti Vari Editi ed Inediti,* Vol. I, Frontispiece. Istituto Poligrafico dello Stato, P.V., Rome, 1957. Figure is referenced as Mogadiscio from the map of Fra Mauro, Cartographer for the Republic of Venice (1460), *Edizione a Cura del Comune di Venezia.*

VIEW OF MOGADISHU. From C. Guillain, *Voyage à la Côte Orientale d'Afrique,* Plate 23. E. Ciceri Lith., Vayot, and A. Bertrand, Editor, Paris, 1856. The figure is referenced as Panorama of Mogadishu, view taken from the terrace of our house. Figure, courtesy Cambridge University Library.

DOOR OF THE MINARET, Al-Ǧami mosque in Mogadishu, from Enrico Cerulli, *Somalia, Scritti Vari Editi ed Inediti,* Vol. I., Fig. III. Istituto Poligrafico dello Stato, P.V., Rome 1957. The Al-Ǧami mosque is the oldest mosque in Mogadishu. The inscription above the door states that the person who built it invokes God's mercy on himself and his parents. The date inscribed is 1 muharram AH 636 [August 14, 1238 AD.]

CORAL STONE HOUSE, Xamar Weyn. Photo Phoebe Ferguson, 1979.

opposite THE OLD PORT, Mogadishu. Photo Manfred Wehrmann.

"...We sailed on from there (Zaila) for fifteen nights and came to Magdashaw
which is a town of enormous size..."

From *The Travels of Ibn Battuta A.D. 1325-1354,* trans. and ed. H.A.R. Gibb.,
Vol. 2. Cambridge University Press. 1962.

TRANSOM FROM A CARVED DOOR on a coral stone house in Xamar Weyn (detail). Photo Manfred Wehrmann.

CARVED WOODEN DOORWAY. Xamar Weyn. Photo Manfred Wehrmann.

From Linda Donley, An overview of research undertaken in Somalia in 1978. The following is an excerpt from a description of a marriage as related by Sheikh Dine Abubakar, an historian from Baraawe:

Weddings generally took place in the home of the groom's family on either Thursday evening or Friday morning. And in the case of a first marriage it always took place on the 14th day of a new moon. If it was the second marriage it took place during the period of no moon.

The night before the wedding the bride was brought to the groom's family home without ceremony.

At the time of the religious ceremony the women from both sides of the family gathered with the bride in the women's room of the house behind a closed door. The men entered the courtyard or central room with the bride groom and *Kadi* and the marriage contract was signed and readings from the Koran recited. After this ceremony the groom went to a specially prepared wedding room *(barzah)* which had a nicely decorated bed and waited until evening for his bride. The bride groom had some of his friends with him to help pass the time and refreshments were served at frequent intervals.

In the evening his friends left and the new bride was brought to him by a servant of the house. The door was shut and locked after the girl entered. The bride was expected to be shy and not talk or show her face which was veiled. The bride groom traditionally gave her a gift of gold jewelry and after some time they got to know each other. As marriages were arranged by the parents this might well be the first time the bride and groom were allowed to see each other.

BEDROOM in the Arabic style at the Somali National Museum, Mogadishu. The Museum was formerly a sultan's palace. Photograph reproduced courtesy of the Fototeca dell 'Istituto Italo-Africano di Roma. Reference Museo della Garese, 3A, Archeologia.

PAINTED DOOR with frame carved in the Azanian style. Collection Tommaso and Mirella Briata, Croce del Sud, Mogadishu. Photo Phoebe Ferguson, 1979.

WINDOW. Xamar Weyn. Wood and iron. H. 70cm, W. 60cm. Collection Anita and Suleiman Adan, Mogadishu. Carved in the Azanian style, the lintel is bordered by a frame with a carved leaf motif. Two small shutters are set into the frame which is decorated with an undulating plait motif. The shutters are carved with encircled eight petal rosettes, half circles, oblique lines, and leaf patterns. The right side of the frame is restored.

CONTEMPORARY LINTEL (detail). Baraawe. Wood. L. 117cm W. 22cm. Collection F.C.C.U., Washington, D.C. Carved in the Azanian style. The center motif is a four-petal aster enclosed in a frame. The carving on this lintel is typical of doorways in Baraawe and Marka.

below WOOD CARVER, working on a trousseau chest. Xamar Weyn. Photo Phoebe Ferguson, 1979.

above TRIVET WITH HANDLE. Baraawe. Carved wood treated with *asal*. D. 18cm. Private Collection. *Asal* is the fiber of a tree treated and fermented to induce a deep reddish color and shine. It is also used to prevent rotting.

below SCRIBE'S CHEST. Mogadishu. Carved wood. L. 59cm, H. 37cm. Collection Giovanni Ferrero, Rome. The crude unfinished outer carvings contrast with the detailed work of the inside compartments and the removeable tray.

above MINIATURE CHAIR. Lamu Island, Kenya. H. 46cm. Wood, fiber and traces of pigment. Collection F.C.C.U., Washington, D.C. The chair was made by a young Somali living on Lamu Island. It is carved of wood with a high rounded back decorated with a heart and leaf motif and bordered by oblique lines. The arms, legs and arm supports are turned in spirals. There are traces of red and green pigment on the chair. The seat is woven of string. The center of the back support is missing.

below THREE LEGGED STAND. Mogadishu. Wood, hide and pigment. H. 42cm. Private Collection. This stand is generally used to support a brass tray for serving coffee or tea and is typical of coastal Somalia.

opposite ROOM, SULTAN'S PALACE, Mogadishu. Intricate plaster work around niches, turned and laquered wooden spindle-posted bed. Photo Crisanne Albers, 1983.

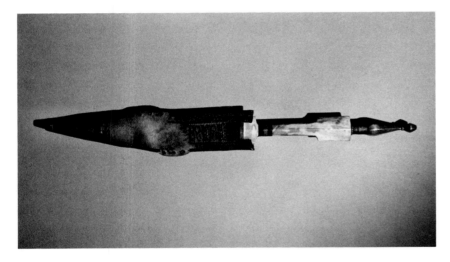

above BOWL with repousse decoration. Xamar Weyn. Brass. H. 10cm. Collection F.C.C.U., Washington, D.C.

below DAGGER AND SCABBARD. Baydhabow. Ivory, brass, horn, silver. L. 46cm. Collection John and Elizabeth Johnson, Bloomington, Indiana. Top of the handle has filigree decorations. The scabbard has geometrical decorations sewn on. This is a nomad's dagger.

COFFEE POT, BOWL AND PLATE.
Coffee pot. Mogadishu. Brass. H. 23cm. Collection F.C.C.U., Washington, D.C. Coffee pots such as these were probably made in Zanzibar by Persian and Omani craftsmen and are found in the coastal towns in Somalia.

Bowl. Mogadishu. Brass. D. 8cm. Collection F.C.C.U., Washington, D.C.

Plate. Mogadishu. Brass and lead. D. 18cm. Private Collection. This sort of plate was imported from India and is typical of the metal plates used in the Southern coastal towns.

above SCRIBE'S CHEST. Mogadishu. Wood with brass inlay, brass handles. L. 39cm, W. 14cm, H. 22cm. Collection Peter and Karin Koch, The Hague.

below BOWL WITH LID. Mogadishu. Copper and tin. H. 17cm, D. 20cm. Collection F.C.C.U., Washington, D.C. The bowl is hammered copper lined with tin.

WOMAN cleaning her hands after a meal. Afgooye. Photo Phoebe Ferguson, 1979.

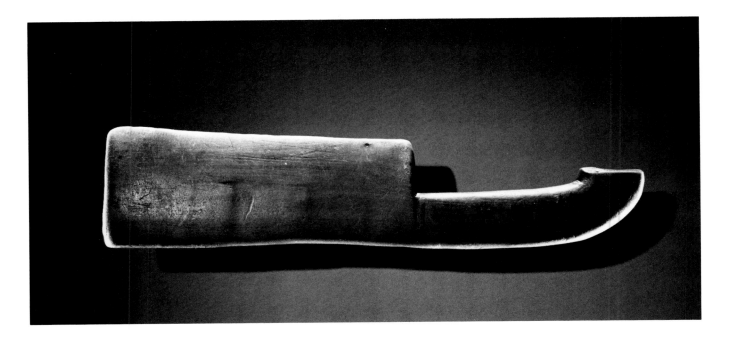

above TOOL. Afgooye. Wood. L. 24cm. Collection John and Elizabeth Johnson, Bloomington, Indiana. This tool is used as a cotton beater in the weaving process. One side bears an Arabic inscription.

below A SOMALI COUPLE. From *The Standard Library of Natural History, Embracing Living Animals and Living Races of Mankind,* Vol. V, Africa—Europe—America, p. 377. The University Society Inc., New York, 1911. The photograph is by Messrs. Negretti and Zambra, London.

above WEAVER in Mogadishu in 1882. From E. Cerulli, *Somalia, Scritti Vari Editi ed Inediti,* Vol. I., Fig. XVII. Istituto Poligrafico dello Stato, P.V., Rome, 1957. Figure is referenced as *Dal Voyage chez les Benadirs* di G. Revoil. Figure courtesy Library of Congress.

below COTTON WEAVING in Mogadishu in 1882. From E. Cerulli, *Somalia, Scritti Vari Editi ed Inediti,* Vol. I., Fig. XVIII. Istituto Poligrafico dello Stato, P.V., Rome, 1957. Figure is referenced as *Dal Voyage chez les Benadirs* di G. Revoil. Figure courtesy Library of Congress.

above BENAADIR WEAVER at the weaver's cooperative in Mogadishu, situated near the market in Xamar Weyn. Traditionally, women spin the cotton and cloth is woven by men. It is mostly produced in Mogadishu and Jelib-Marka and represents an important industry in the coastal areas. Photo Phoebe Ferguson, 1979.

below PILE OF BENAADIR CLOTH at the weaver's cooperative market. Xamar Weyn. The original *futa Benaadir* was white. Multicolored yarns were introduced in the late 1800's. Photo Phoebe Ferguson, 1979.

opposite GROUP OF WOMEN wearing Benaadir cloth, Northern Somalia. Photo Phoebe Ferguson, 1979.

"...All small articles are exchanged for beads,
but sheep and cattle are paid for in cotton cloth,
the former costing one tobe and the latter eight..."

From *The Unknown Horn of Africa: An Exploration
from Berbera to the Leopold River* by F. L. James,
George Philip and Son Pub., London, 1888.

SPOONS, *fandhal*. Baydhabow. Wood. L. 27cm and 22cm respectively. Collection F.C.C.U., Washington, D.C. Carved in Azanian style with plaited patterns and cross hatching. Spoons such as these are used on festive occasions to serve roasted coffee beans.

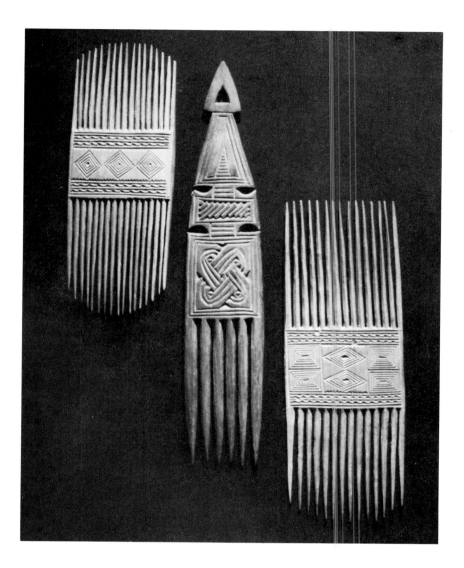

COMBS, *saqaf* or *shanleh*. Baraawe. Wood. L. 27cm, 22cm, and 18cm respectively. Collection F.C.C.U., Washington, D.C.

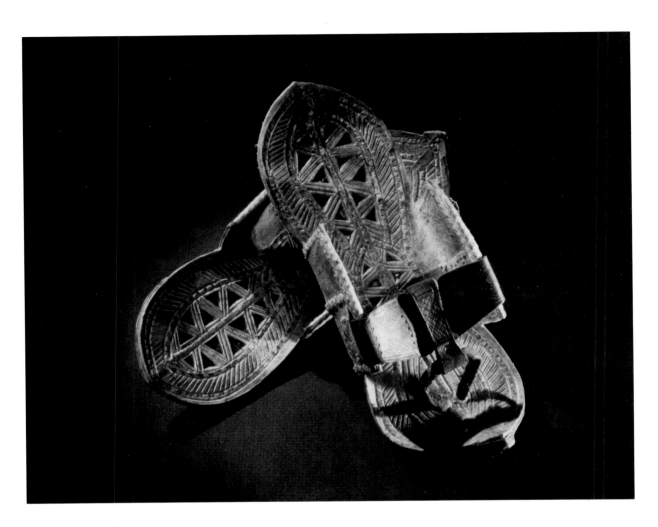

above PAIR OF SANDALS, *kabo.* Baydhabow. Repousse and incised camel leather. L. 25cm. Collection F.C.C.U Washington, D.C.

below WOMAN stretching skins for drying. Ceerigaabo Photo Manfred Wehrmann.

TRADITIONAL STOOL AND PAIR OF SANDALS. Mogadishu. The stool is made of stretched goatskin. The wooden sandals, *kabo,* have tooled leather strappings and twisted leather tow strings. Collection Somali National Museum, Mogadishu. Photo Phoebe Ferguson, 1979.

I am like a sailing ship dragged by a storm
I set my compass towards a place empty of people

Excerpt from a poem by an anonymous poet

FISHING BOATS in Marka. Photo Phoebe Ferguson, 1979.

opposite TWO FISHERMEN going out to sea. Baraawe.
Photo Manfred Wehrmann.

Fish will not die in a Mars-linked disaster or in drought
Nor in the weather of the hot Khaliil season
For the man who has the skill to catch it,
And who knows the ways of the sea
There is wealth there, equally for the rich and the poor

Excerpt from a poem by Faarax M.J. Cawl

MAN AND CHILD repairing fishing traps in Jasiira. Photo
Manfred Wehrmann.

opposite FISHERMAN bringing in his catch. Marka. Photo
Phoebe Ferguson, 1979.

above MARKET PLACE in Mogadishu. Photo Phoebe Ferguson, 1979.

below TRANSPORTATION near the Lido, Mogadishu. Photo Phoebe Ferguson, 1979.

WATCHMAN at the Museum in Hargeysa. Photo Phoebe Ferguson, 1979.

THE MOSQUE of Abd Al-Aziz and the Mnāra tower in Mogadishu in 1882. From E. Cerulli, *Somalia, Scritti Vari Editi ed Inediti,* Vol. I. Fig. XVI. Istituto Poligrafico dello Stato, P.V. Rome 1957. Figure is referenced as *Dal Voyage chez les Benadirs* di G. Revoil. Figure courtesy Library of Congress.

ISLAM IN SOMALIA

I. M. Lewis

The Somalis are Sunni Muslims, following the Shafi'i rite of the Shariah. Since its introduction in the first centuries of the Islamic era by immigrant Arabs who developed such ancient coastal centers as Zeila (in the north) and Mogadishu (in the south), the Somalis have demonstrated a profound dedication to the Muslim faith. Somali culture is permeated by Islam, and, especially in distinction to Christian Ethiopia, the Islamic religion has become strongly identified with Somali sentiments of national identity. At the same time, and in no way detracting from their commitment to Islam, Somali culture and society strongly affect the character and modalities of the local style of Muslim life. The exacting role of women in herd management in the nomadic economy is hardly consistent with any rigid seclusion, and except in some cases in towns, women rarely are seen veiled. Similarly, the most pervasive distinction in Somali society after that of gender is between the religious (e.g., *wadaad*) and the laiety (*waranleh,* lit. "spear-bearer"). The former is the Somali term for the religious specialist known in Arabic as *Shaikh* (a word used synonymously), and the latter refers to all those (the majority) who are not trained in religion and traditionally bear arms for defense and offense. This dichotomy reflects the political and social realities of a traditionally strife-ridden society, with religious specialists mediating between feuding warrior clans, as well as, of course, between men and God. In the former process, compensation for death and injuries was regulated, on a collective basis, in terms of the standard Islamic *diya* (blood-money) tariff.

Other regional differences in the character of Somali society also find their reflection in the local practice of Islam. The northern Somali pastoral nomads are, traditionally, organized into an elaborate system of clans and lineages.[1] In the region between the Shebelle and Juba rivers in the south, however, where the subsistence emphasis shifts from pastoral nomadism to cultivation, and the population includes Oromo and Bantu elements, lineage ties are less prominent. Here the political organization of tribal groups, which are typically coalitions, is primarily territorial, with less stress on common genealogical descent.[2] These regional variations in social and political structure are reflected in the different constitution of the Muslim cult of saints in the two regions. Among the northern nomads, lineage ancestors are virtually automatically transformed into Sufi saints and incorporated into the general cult of Muslim saints, which, of course, includes those international figures —such as Sheikh Abdul Qadir al-Jilani—famous throughout the Islamic world. In the south there is no corresponding structural "canonization" of lineage ancestors. There are local saints, but they are venerated for their own personal piety and religious efficacy rather than for, as it were, sociological reasons.[3] Thus, the Somalis have enthusiastically adopted Islam and, over the centuries, adapted it to their own particular needs. There remains a perennial tension, resolved in certain contexts, between the internal conflicts of this traditionally warrior culture and the ideally pacific, international values of Islamic solidarity.

The cult of saints—the Sufi mystical movement in Islam—seems, as we have seen, generally well suited to the predominantly kinship character of Somali society. Saints provide the hope of direct mediation between man and the Prophet and ultimately God, and trust in them is to some extent a reflection of a sense of human impotence and spiritual inadequacy. The profession of the faith has, thus, for Somalis tended to be synonymous with adherence to one or another of the main Sufi religious orders, usually the Qaadiriya (associated locally with the ancient Islamic center of Harar), or, since its introduction in the early nineteenth century, the Ahmadiya and its branches (especially the Salihiya). Mosques usually are associated with one or another of these orders—although some are interdenominational. Most teachers of Islam also belong to a particular order, although the most famous early pillar of Islam, Sharif Yusuf Aw Barkhadle (the 'Blessed Saint'),[4] probably a twelfth-century figure, antedates the brotherhoods. Sharif Yusuf, who left no physical descendants, transcends the Somali clan structure and is the most powerful of all local saints. To go three times in pilgrimage to his shrine is considered of equal religious merit to going once to Mecca. Sharif Yusuf is credited with the invention of a Somali notation for the Arabic short vowels, which is still followed today, in rural religious schools, where, using wooden tablets as blackboards, children learn the rudiments of the Qoran and of religion generally. The main students were boys, temporarily released from herding duties in the pastoral economy to attend these itinerant religious schools, whose teachers were paid in kind according to the number of chapters in the Qoran learned by their pupils. Literacy in Arabic was always very limited.

In addition to teaching Islam and Arabic, mediating between warring clans, and administering the Shariah in family contexts, these religious specialists also provided supernatural remedies for illness and affliction. A characteristic treatment consisted in the administration to the sick of a draft prepared by washing a handwritten passage from the Qoran into a cup filled with water. This literal imbibing of holy writ can be seen as the triumphant incorporation of the Arabic literate tradition within the oral Somali tradition. Arabic has always been treated as the unique religious vehicle, existing alongside the dominant oral Somali tradition with its extraordinarily rich poetic heritage,[5] closely paralleling the division between religious (wadaad) and lay (waranleh).

If religion seems historically, in this culture, a natural adjunct and complement to lay society, as might be expected, the two spheres have achieved their most successful fusion in the context of "holy war" *(jihad).* Here the local tradition goes back to the fourteenth century, when the Sultan of Ifat (or Awdal, whose port was Zeila) launched a Muslim crusade against Christian Ethiopia. The pinnacle of Islamic success was achieved in 1540 with the short-lived conquest of central Ethiopia by the victorious armies led by the fiery Muslim champion Ahmad Ibrahim Al-Ghazi (or "Gran," or "Guray" the left-handed) in 1540. Gran's defeat near Lake Tana in 1542 signaled the decline of Islamic political fortunes in the long and bitter history of conflict between the Christian Ethiopians and the surrounding Muslim sultanates.[6] Somali clansmen, renowned for their skill as "cutters of roads," played a significant part here, and one of their most famous leaders was a namesake of Imam Ahmad. It is thus not surprising that these two figures should have become fused in the Somali oral tradition and find their modern, physical embodiment in the statue *Ahmad Guray,* prominently displayed in Somalia's capital, Mogadishu.

A more recent and indubitably Somali hero in this tradition is Sayyid Mohamad 'Abdille Hassan, who led the celebrated *jihad* against the Christian colonizers of his country from 1900 to 1920. Its onset coincided with the first impress of imperial rule, triggered by the Ethiopian emperor Menelik's military excursions into the Ogaden. Although he lived with his mother's people in the LasAnod region, Sayyid Mohamad himself belonged to the Ogaden clan. His religious affiliation was to the Salihiya brotherhood (a derivative of the Ahmadiya), and one of his sources of inspiration was the Sudanese Mahdi. He was also a strong opponent of the entrenched Qadariya Order, which he regarded as conservative and reactionary and whose leaders (one of whom was assassinated by his followers) violently denounced him. Sayyid Mohamad's immediate enemies, however, against whom the call to *jihad* was declared, were the Ethiopian and British colonizers of Northern Somalia: the French at Jibuti remained beyond his range of operations, and the Italians to the south played, for the most part, a relatively minor role. Making consummate use of all the traditional tricks of Somali clan politics and of his remarkable skills in rhetoric and poetry, Sayyid Mohamad indomitably led his "Dervishes" through four major colonial military expeditions. It was only in 1920, when aircraft were used for the first time to bomb African "insurgents," that his movement finally disintegrated; the Sayyid himself died of influenza at Imi in the Ogaden.[7] Although this "holy war" against foreign intrusion was waged in the name and under the banner of Islam by a learned sheikh, the power of the Somali *oral* tradition is clearly reflected in the extent to which Sayyid Mohamad's success depended directly on his brilliant mastery of the Somali art of polemic poetry.[8] It is significant that he is remembered most widely today first as a poet and second as a pioneering figure in the development of modern Somali national consciousness.

The mobilizing power of the *jihad* in this traditional nationalist context has been invoked in the recent Somali/Ethiopian war of 1977/78 by the Western Somali Liberation Front freedom fighters and their allies. It also has been employed by General Mohamad Siyad Barre's government to mobilize popular support for such modern programs as rural development and mass literacy in the Somali vernacular (with the Roman script as medium).[9] In the same reforming spirit, in 1978 the "Somali family law" was imposed, despite the protests of some traditional religious leaders, to increase women's inheritance rights (rarely fully honored where livestock are involved) and their legal position in divorce, and to curtail polygyny.

The official Somali Women's Democratic Organization exists to safeguard women's interests and to promote further reforms, including the abolition of the traditional practice of female circumcision. Its manifesto, significantly, condemns those forms of spirit possession (*saar, mingis,* etc.)[10] which have been resorted to by urban housewives, to combat their husbands' efforts to impose stricter Islamic seclusion than that customary in the nomadic interior. Historically, the rise of these "pagan" spirit cults (which are actually *post-* rather than *pre-*Islamic) correlates closely with urbanization, a process which may lead to a decline, rather than improvement, in women's rights. The attraction of such cults is also a measure of the exclusion of women from full participation in Islamic ritual. The implication, manifestly, is that as the freedom of women in urban society increases rather than decreases in comparison with the traditional nomadic pattern, so such subterfuge strategies will become redundant.

THE FAKHR AD-DĪN MOSQUE in Mogadishu in 1882. From E. Cerulli, *Somalia, Scritti Vari Editi ed Inediti,* Vol. I, Fig. XV. Istituto Poligrafico dello Stato, P.V. Rome, 1957. The Figure is referenced as *Dal Voyage chez les Benadirs* di G. Revoil. The Fakhr ad-Dīn mosque is situated between Xamar Weyn and the Sheikh Muumin quarters of Mogadishu. Figure courtesy Library of Congress.

"O ye faithful, come to prayer.
O ye faithful, come to the house of God."

Proverb

left THE MNĀRA TOWER, Mogadishu. Photo Ali Abdi Adaue, 1970.

right CONTEMPORARY MOSQUE, Mogadishu. Photo Phoebe Ferguson, 1979.

opposite PILGRIMS at the tomb of Sufi Saint Uways Ma-ḥammad. Biyooley, Northwest of Baydhabow. Photo Said Sheikh Samatar, 1977.

LEARNING TABLETS, *loox*. Mogadishu. Yucub wood and charcoal ink. H. 68cm, 68cm, and 99cm respectively. Collection F.C.C.U., Washington, D.C. These tablets are used by children in Koranic schools.

opposite CHILDREN with their wooden tablets at a Koranic School in Southern Somalia. Children start Koranic school between the age of 4 and 6. The tablets they use are made of thin slivers of wood. They are taught to write the ancient Islamic kufi script with a flat nibbed writing instrument. The ink is made of a mixture of coal dust and water or coal dust and milk and sugar. Photo Manfred Wehrmann.

O God teach me Your Word on a writing board

Traditional prayer

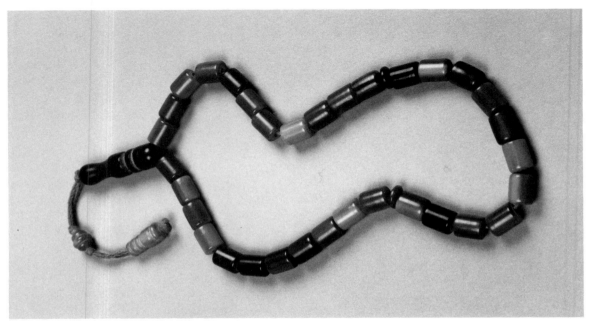

WATER VESSEL WITH STOPPER, *weyso.* Mogadishu. Carved wood with undulating plait pattern. H. 28cm, D. 45cm. Collection Abby Thomas, Washington, D.C. Used throughout Somalia, wooden water vessels such as these are for ablutions. The word, *weyso,* means to wash for prayer.

opposite above left PITCHER WITH LONG SLENDER SPOUT. Mogadishu. Silver and alloy. H. 20cm. Collection Martin and Evelyn Ganzglass, Washington, D.C. This pitcher is used for ablutions.

opposite above right ROSEWATER BOTTLE WITH CAP. Xamar Weyn. Glass and silver. Bottle H. 21½cm, Cap H. 8cm. Collection National Museum of African Art, Washington, D.C. Rosewater is traditionally used for ablutions.

opposite below PRAYER BEADS. Mogadishu. Semi-precious stones. L. 30cm. Collection John and Elizabeth Johnson, Bloomington, Indiana. These prayer beads are usually carried by Moslem men. These beads might have been imported from the Middle East.

I shall satisfy your craving, as when one pours out salty water for a she-camel
I shall entertain you with a poem as precious as a jewel

Excerpt from a poem by Sayid Mohammed Abdille Hassan

NECKLACE WITH CRESCENT PENDANT. Xamar Weyn. Amber, agate and silver. L. 60cm. 18th century. Private Collection. Large amber beads, *asli,* and pendant of silver repousse work decorated with silver bells and agate stones. For centuries amber has been prized not only for its beauty but for its medicinal and magical qualities as well.

opposite PORTE KORAN, *xirsi.* Xamar Weyn. Silver, amber and red beads. L. 50cm. 19th century. Collection F.C.C.U., Washington, D.C. Open work and applique work dependant on a necklace of amber, faceted silver and red beads with silver trumpet ends.

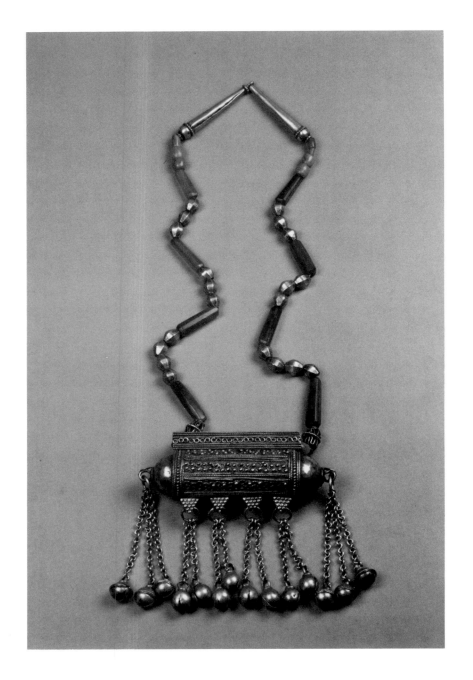

TUBULAR PORTE KORAN, *xirsi*. Afgooye. Silver. L. 76cm. Collection Virginia Luling, London. Applique and filigree work with chains and bells, *shanuuf,* dependant from a necklace of alternating faceted agate and silver beads, with coral and semi-precious stones, applique trumpet ends, *bes-bees. Bes-bees* means hot pepper.

opposite RECTANGULAR PORTE KORAN, *xirsi*. Bosaaso. Silver. L. 84cm. Collection F.C.C.U., Washington, D.C. Applique, filigree and repousse work, dependant from a chain belt with applique medallions and large "S" shaped clasp. A small paper bearing verses from the Koran is placed in the rectangular box as an amulet for the protection of the wearer. These amulets can be worn on the arm, around the neck or waist, or hung on the wall. The word *xirsi* means protection.

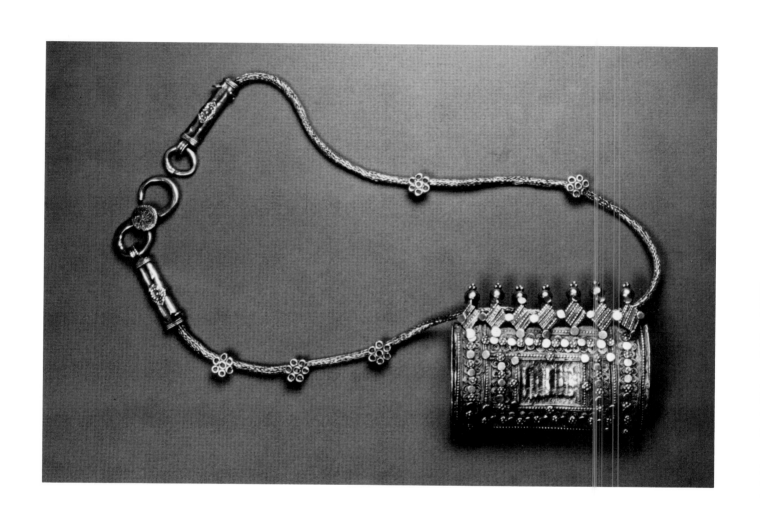

O God, let my amulet be fashioned only by you

Traditional blessing

above RECTANGULAR PORTE KORAN, *xirsi.* Xamar Weyn. Silver, agate, and amber. L. 61cm. 18th century. Private Collection. Applique work with center flower motif and leaf borders hanging from a necklace of amber, agate and silver beads and bangles. This type of necklace is worn throughout Somalia.

below TUBULAR PORTE KORAN, *xirsi.* Jennali. Silver. L. 58cm. 18th century. Collection F.C.C.U., Washington, D.C. Herringbone engraving, applique work with chains, bells and bangles dependant from a link chain.

opposite WOMAN wearing Porte Koran, *hersi,* with small child, Northern Somalia. Photo Phoebe Ferguson, 1979.

WEDDING NECKLACE, *muriyad.* Marka. Silver. L. 42cm. 18th century. Collection F.C.C.U., Washington, D.C. Unusual filigree ball and coiled metal trumpet ends, bes-bees. This necklace may have come from a sultan's family. Given to a bride by her husband, a wedding necklace remains her property for life. In the instance of a divorce, if a husband would ask for the return of the necklace he would be frowned upon by the community. In one Somali poem, a mother says that she will give up her necklace to aid her daughter in trouble.

PORTE KORAN, *xirsi*. Xamar Weyn. Silver. L. 72cm. 18th century. Collection F.C.C.U., Washington, D.C. Filigree and diamond shaped applique work with chains and bells, *shanuuf,* dependant from a circular link chain.

above BATH SANDALS. Baraawe. Silver and wood. L. 27cm. Private Collection. The wooden form is entirely covered with silver. Sandals of this type are rare and are usually worn by a bridegroom. They are similar to those worn in Yemen and India.

below BRACELET, *birmad.* Bosaaso. Silver with red stone. D. 8cm. Collection F.C.C.U., Washington, D.C. This bracelet is worn on the upper arm during dances performed the last day of healing rites in a women's society.

TIERED COMB, *saqaf* or *shanleh*. Xamar Weyn. Silver. L. 25cm. 18th century. Collection F.C.C.U., Washington, D.C. Comb decorated with applique and filigree work, three bells on the top. This type of comb is usually given to a bride by her mother or grandmother. It is called a *saqaf* in the north and a *shanleh* in the south.

WOMAN wearing both the *shilingi* and *labad* necklaces in the traditional manner of Southern Somalia. Photograph reproduced courtesy of the Fototeca dell'Istituto Italo-Africano di Roma. Reference No. 8850.

above CHOKER NECKLACE, *labad.* Xamar Weyn. Gold. L. 21cm. 18th century. Collection F.C.C.U., Washington, D.C. Rectangular sections with diamond shaped links, square section and two triangular end pieces. This type of necklace is generally worn in southern Somalia along with the *shilingi* necklace.

below PENDANTS AND BEADS from a *shilingi* necklace (detail). Xamar Weyn. Gold. L. 50cm. 18th century. Collection F.C.C.U., Washington, D.C. Necklace of ball beads, faceted beads and open work beads, four repousse and filigree medallions, a central crescent shaped pendant and trumpet ends.

above CHOKER NECKLACE, *laasin.* Xamar Weyn. Gold. L. 28cm. 19th century. Private Collection. Triple strand beads separated by rectangular sections with large round beads in the center of the necklace. This type of necklace is generally worn in southern Somalia and can be worn with the wedding necklace.

below ARMLET, *dugaagad.* Xamar Weyn. Gold. D. 20cm. 18th century. Private Collection. Hollow armlet from which hangs a repousse and applique work amulet. It is usually worn on the upper arm.

WEDDING NECKLACE, *muriyad.* Xamar Weyn. Gold and gomma lacca. L. 80 cm. 18th century. Private Collection. Double strand of alternating round and faceted beads, repousse work and trumpet ends.

above PAIR OF CHILD'S BRACELETS, *waqafyo*. Xamar Weyn.
Silver. 18th century. Private Collection. Applique and
filigree work.

below ARMLET, *dugaagad* Bosaaso. Silver. D. 12cm. 19th
century. Private Collection. Intricate filigree, chains and
six repousse bells.

above ANKLET, *hujuul.* Xamar Weyn. Silver. D. 18cm. Early 19th century. Collection F.C.C.U., Washington, D.C. Repousse bells with applique work and diamond shaped ends, floral applique clasp with chain and bar closure. The bells are generally made of an alloy with a lesser amount of silver than the anklet to insure a melodic ring. This type of anklet is worn for dancing at weddings and other festive occasions.

below ANKLETS, *hujuul.* Photo reproduced courtesy of the Fototeca dell'Istituto Italo-Africano di Roma. Reference Bracciale, 2/K Artigianato.

left PAIR OF KOHL POTS AND STICKS. Xamar Weyn. Silver. H. 14cm. 19th century. Collection F.C.C.U., Washington, D.C. Ball and tube pots with repousse work, chains and engraved sticks. Kohl, a very fine dark colored powder, is ground from a stone. It is said to have a soothing property which cleanses the eyes, keeps evil spirits away, and protects the eyes from the sun. *Kuul* is the Somali word for kohl.

right TWO KOHL STICKS. Xamar Weyn. Silver. L. 10cm and 12cm. respectively. 19th century. Collection F.C.C.U., Washington, D.C.

KOHL POT WITH LID AND STICK. Xamar Weyn. Silver. L. 14cm. 18th century. Collection F.C.C.U., Washington, D.C. Old saddle bag design with bangle bells. Kohl pots are usually a gift to the bride from her mother or grandmother. The kohl pots will often be presented in embroidered and decorated cloth cases.

NOTES

Johnson: *Introduction*

1. The reader will note a variety of spelling usage in this catalogue, which is due to the fact that until a decade ago, there was no official orthography for the writing of Somali. Today, a modified Latin alphabet is officially employed in Somalia, modified in that some Latin characters which represent sounds not in the Somali language are employed for sounds not represented by Latin characters. "X," for example, is used for a pharyngeal sound often written with an "H" when Arabic is transliterated into Latin spelling. "C" is the official Somali spelling for the "'ayn"; thus, while many readers are used to seeing the name *Ali* spelled without regard to this sound at all, or with a raised comma as *'Ali,* Somalis spell it *Cali.* Some of the essayists in this catalogue chose to adopt the official Somali orthography, and some chose the older, less accurate but, to foreigners, more recognizable conventions. Therefore, the Somali name *Maxamad* (spelled thus in the Somali script) is also spelled as *Muḥammad* and *Mohamed* in various essays. The editors have chosen not to tamper with the choices of individual essayists. We have, however, used the official orthography for photo captions and object descriptions. The following brief description should help to clarify Somali spelling usage. Most of the characters in the Somali orthography represent the same or nearly the same sounds represented by that character in Latin. The following exceptions represent sounds for which Latin has no symbol:
    <x> = voiceless pharyngeal similar to [ḥ] in Arabic
    <c> = voiced pharyngeal similar to [ʕ] in Arabic
    <q> = postpalatal voiceless stop, similar to [q] in Arabic
    <dh> = retroflexed postalveolar voiced stop similar to [ḍ] in Sanskrit
    <kh> = palatal voiceless fricative, similar to [x] in Arabic
    <'> = glottal stop, similar to "t" in mountain, thus [ʔ]
        long vowels are indicated by the doubling of the letter
    For the history behind the adoption of a modifed Latin script for Somali, see B.W. Andrzejewski, "The Introduction of a National Orthography for Somali," *African Language Studies* 15 (1974): 199-203.

Arnoldi: *The Artistic Heritage of Somalia*

1. Editor's Note: "The Artistic Heritage of Somalia" first appeared in *African Arts* 7 no. 4 (August 1984): 24-33, 93. It has been slightly edited for republication here.

2. Margaret Castagno, *Historical Dictionary of Somalia* (Metuchen, N.J.: Scarecrow Press, 1975), pp. 48, 128.

3. Ibid., p. 14.

4. Lee Cassanelli, *The Shaping of Somali Society: Reconstructing the History of a Pastoral People, 1600-1900* (Philadelphia: University of Pennsylvania Press, 1982), p. 9.

5. Gervase Mathew, "Chinese Porcelain in East Africa and on the Coast of South Arabia," *Oriental Art,* n.s. 2 (1956), p. 52.

6. Ibn Battuta, *The Travels of Ibn Battuta,* A.D. *1325-1354* (London: Cambridge University Press, 1962), vol. 2, pp. 373-75.

7. Henry Yule, *Cathay and the Way Thither* (1915; reprint ed., Taipei: Ch'eng-Wen Pub. Co., 1966), vol. 1, p. 87, n. 1.

8. Cassanelli, *Somali Society,* p. 152.

9. Ibn Battuta, *Travels,* pp. 373-74.

10. I.M. Lewis, *Peoples of the Horn of Africa,* 2d ed. (London: International African Institute, 1969), p. 46.

11. Ibid., p. 41.

12. Cassanelli, *Somali Society,* pp. 191-92.

13. Ibid., p. 148, n. 2.

14. Enrico Cerulli, *Scritti vari editi ed inediti* (Rome: Amministrazione Fiduciaria Italiana della Somalia, 1959), vol. 2, pp. 1-18.

15. Richard Burton, *First Footsteps in East Africa* (New York: Praeger, 1966), p. 93.

16. John William Johnson, *Heellooy Heelleellooy: The Development of the Genre Heello in Modern Somali Poetry* (Bloomington, Ind.: Research Center for the Language Sciences, 1974).

17. Said Sheikh Samatar, *Oral Poetry and Somali Nationlism: The Case of Sayyid Moḥammad 'Abdille Ḥassan* (Cambridge: Cambridge University Press, 1982).

18. Nello Puccioni, *Resultati scientifici delle Missioni Stefanini Paoli (1913) et Stefanini—Puccioni (1924) en Somalia* (New Haven: Human Relations Area Files, 1960), pp. 4-5.

19. Ibid., p. 36.

20. Ibid., pp. 50-51.

21. Ibid., pp. 22-24.

22. Personal communication: John William Johnson, 1984.

23. Cerulli, *Scritti vari,* vol. 2, pp. 92-93.

24. Unpublished translation by B.W. Andrzejewski, 1982.

25. Ibid.

26. Vinigi Grottanelli, "Somali Wood Engravings," *African Arts* 1, no. 3 (1968).

27. Ibid., p. 9.

28. Lewis, *Peoples,* p. 78.

29. Ibid., p. 84.

30. Ibn Battuta, *Travels,* p. 374.

31. Cassanelli, *Somali Society,* p. 167.

32. Virginia Luling, "The Social Structure of Southern Somali Tribes" (Ph.D. diss., University of London, 1971).

33. Puccioni, *Resultati,* p. 5; personal communication: Virginia Luling, 1983.

34. Puccioni, *Resultati,* pp. 61-65.

35. Ibid., p. 49.

36. Desmond Clark, "Dancing Masks from Somaliland," *Man* 53, no. 72 (1953): 49-51.

37. Ibid., p. 51.

Samatar: *Somali Verbal and Material Arts*

1. Some material in this article has been drawn from Said Sheikh Samatar, *Oral Poetry and Somali Nationalism: The Case of Sayyid Moḥammad 'Abdille Ḥasan* (Cambridge: Cambridge University Press, 1982).

Andrzejewski: *The Literary Culture of the Somali People*

1. See W.H. Auden, *A Certain World: A Commonplace Book* (London: Faber and Faber, 1970); Ruth Finnegan, ed., *A World Treasury of Oral Poetry* (Bloomington: Indiana University Press, 1978); Alan Lomax and Raoul Abdul, eds., *3000 Years of Black Poetry* (New York: Dodd, Mead & Co., 1970); and W.H. Whiteley, ed., *A Selection of African Prose* (Oxford: Clarendon Press, 1964).

2. See Ruth Finnegan, *Oral Literature in Africa* (Oxford: Clarendon Press, 1970); Albert Gérard, *African Language Literatures: An Introduction to the Literary History of Sub-Saharan Africa* (Harlow, England; Longman, 1981); and *Ungar's Encyclopedia of World Literature in the 20th Century,* 2d ed. rev. (New York: Frederick Ungar Pub. Co., 1984).

3. A discussion of the issues involved can be found in Ruth Finnegan, *Oral Poetry: Its Nature, Significance, and Social Context* (Cambridge: Cambridge University Press, 1977), and John William Johnson, "Recent Contributions by Somalis and Somalists to the Study of Oral Literature," in *Somalia and the World: Proceedings of the International Symposium Held in Mogadishu, October 15-21, 1979,* ed. Hussein M. Adam (Mogadishu, Somalia: *Halgan* Editorial Board, 1980), vol. 1, pp. 117-31.

4. Enrico Cerulli, *Somalia: Scritti vari editi ed inediti* (Rome: Instituti Poligrafico dello Stato, 1964), vol. 3, pp. 118-38.

5. Information about this type of poetry can be found in John William Johnson, "The Family of Miniature Genres in Somali Oral Poetry," *Folklore Forum* 5, no. 3 (1972): 79-99, and in Omar Au Nuh, *Some General Notes on Somali Folklore* (Mogadishu: Author, 1970); examples of texts are also available in B.W. Andrzejewski and I.M. Lewis, *Somali Poetry: An Introduction* (Oxford: Clarendon Press, 1964).

6. Examples of this type of prose can be found in Mohamed Farah Abdullahi, *The Best Stories from the Land of Punt (Somalia)* (Mogadishu: Author, 1970); Margaret Laurence, *A Tree for Poverty: Somali Poetry and Prose* (Shannon: Irish University Press, 1970); and Whiteley, *African Prose.*

7. Some texts of this kind are provided in the collections of stories listed in note 6.

8. Information on these three legends and illustrative texts are provided in B.W. Andrzejewski, "The Veneration of Sufi Saints and its Impact on the Oral Literature of the Somali People and Their Literature in Arabic," *African Language Studies* 15 (1974): 15-53.

9. The most extensive account of this type of poetry, well illustrated with texts and up to date in relation to recent research, is found in the second chapter (pp. 55-90) of Said Sheikh Samatar, *Oral Poetry and Somali Nationalism: The Case of Sayyid Maḥammad 'Abdille Ḥassan* (Cambridge: Cambridge University Press, 1982). Further information and texts can be found in B.W. Andrzejewski, "Poetry in Somali Society," in *Sociolinguistics: Selected Readings,* ed. J.B. Pride and Janet Holms (Harmondsworth: Penguin Books, 1972), pp. 252-59; B.W. Andrzejewski, "The Poem as Message: Verbatim Memorization in Somali Poetry," in *Memory and Poetic Structure: Papers on the Conference on Oral Literature and Literary Theory Held at Middlesex Polytechnic, 1981* (London: Middlesex Polytechnic, 1981), pp. 1-25; B.W. Andrzejewski, "Voices from the Horn of Africa," *Ur: The International Magazine of Arab Culture,* 2, no. 3 (1982): 28-29; Andrzejewski and Lewis, *Somali Poetry;* B.W. Andrzejewski and Musa H.I. Galaal, "A Somali Poetic Combat," *Journal of African Languages* 2, no. 1 (1963): 15-28, 2, no. 2 (1963): 93-100, and 2, no. 3 (1963): 190-205; Laurence, *A Tree for Poverty;* and Said Sheikh Samatar, "Gabay-ḥayir: A Somali Mock Heroic Song," *Research in African Literatures* 11, no. 4 (1980): 449-78.

10. The original text of this poem is found in Shire Jaamac Achmed, *Gabayo, maahmaah, iyo sheekooyin yaryar* (Mogadishu: National Printers, 1965), p. 46. I have adapted the original transcription to conform with the official orthography and to represent the normal flow of speech.

11. The results of this discovery were first described in a series of articles in Somali in the national daily *Xiddigta Oktoobar* in 1976-78, and were made accessible outside Somalia through an article by John William Johnson, "Somali Prosodic Systems," *Horn of Africa* 2, no. 3 (1979): 46-54, where substantial further advances in the analysis were offered. The data contained in this article were updated and substantially corrected in John William Johnson, "Recent Researches into the Scansion of Somali Oral Poetry," in *Proceedings of the Second International Congress of Somali Studies, University of Hamburg August 1-6, 1983,* ed. Thomas Labahn (Hamburg: Helmut Buske Verlag, 1984), pp. 313-31. More information can be found in Abdillahi Deria Guled, "The Scansion of Somali Poetry," in *Somalia and the World.*

12. The use of poetry in the war of the Dervishes is described in detail in Said Sheikh Samatar, *Oral Poetry and Somali Nationalism*. Further information can be found in Andrzejewski and Lewis, *Somali Poetry*. The name of the leader of the Dervishes, Sayid Maxamed Cabdulle Xasan, is spelled differently by various authors as Sayyid Maḥammad 'Abdille Ḥassan, Sayid Mohamed Abdille Hassan, Sayyid Mohamed Abdullah Hassan, etc.

13. The original text of this poem is taken from M.H.I. Galaal, ed., *A Collection of Somali Literature: Mainly from Sayid Mohamed Abdille Hassan* (Mogadishu: Author, c. 1964), p. 3.

14. Texts of poems of this type are available in Andrzejewski and Galaal, "A Somali Poetic Combat." The name of Musa H.I. Galaal, a well-known Somali scholar, appears in different forms in various publications. The most common variants are Muuse Xaaji Ismaaciil Galaal, Musa H.I. Galaal, and Muusa Galaal.

15. Information about this poet and translations about some of his works can be found in Laurence, *A Tree for Poverty*, and in Mohamed Farah Abdillahi and B.W. Andrzejewski, "The Life of 'Ilmi Bowndheri, a Somali Poet Who Is Said to Have Died of Love," *Journal of the Folklore Institute* 4, no. 2/3 (1967): 191-206. Cilmi Bowndheri, 'Ilmi Bowndheri, and Elmi Bonderii are spelling variants of the same name. The last of these is used in Margaret Laurence's book.

16. The original text of this poem is found in Rashiid Maxamed Shabeele, *Ma dhabba jacayl waa loo dhintaa* (Xamar [Mogadishu]: Maxbacadda Qaranka, 1975), p. 67.

17. This type of poetry is described in B.W. Andrzejewski, "The Art of the Miniature in Somali Poetry," *African Language Review* 6 (1967): 5-16; and in John William Johnson, *Heellooy Heelleellooy: The Development of the Genre Heello in Modern Somali Poetry* (Bloomington, Ind.: Research Center for the Language Sciences, 1974).

18. The work of Somali scholars who contributed to the preservation of Somali literature is described in the following publications: B.W. Andrzejewski, "The Rise of Written Somali Literature," *African Research and Documentation* 8/9 (1975): 7-14; B.W. Andrzejewski, "The Somali Academy of Culture," *I.A.I. Bulletin: African Studies Notes and News* 46, no. 1, supplement to *Africa* (1977): 6-7; B.W. Andrzejewski, "The Survival of the National Culture in Somalia during and after the Colonial Era: the Contribution of Poets, Playwrights, and Collectors of Oral Literature," *N.E.A. Journal of Research on North East Africa* 1, no. 1 (1981): 3-15; B.W. Andrzejewski, "Muuse Xaaji Ismaaciil Galaal (1914-1980): A Founding Father of Written Somali," *Horn of Africa* 4, no. 2 (1981): 21-25; and John William Johnson, "Research in Somali Folklore," *Research in African Literatures* 4, no. 1 (1973): 51-61. Note that the earlier name of the Academy of Arts and Sciences was the Academy of Culture.

19. Extensive information on this type of poetry and its social and political aspects is available in Johnson, *Heellooy Heelleellooy*, and in Abdisalam Yassin Mohamed, "Political Themes and Imagery in Modern Somali Poetry" (B.A. thesis, Vermont College, 1973).

20. The original text of this poem is taken from B.W. Andrzejewski's private collection of transcripts of oral literature.

21. The text of this poem is available in Johnson, *Heellooy Heelleellooy*, pp. 93-94.

22. Both the original text and the translation are taken from ibid., pp. 140-42. The conference referred to took place in 1984-85.

23. The literary characteristics of Somali drama and its stagecraft techniques are described in the introduction to Hassan Sheikh Mumin, *Leopard among the Women: Shabeelnaagood: A Somali Play* (London: Oxford University Press, 1974), translated with an introduction by B.W. Andrzejewski. An account of the relationship between Somali drama and folklore is given in B.W. Andrzejewski, "Modern and Traditional Aspects of Somali Drama," in *Folklore in the Modern World*, ed. Richard Dorson (The Hague: Mouton, 1978), pp. 87-101.

24. Information about written literature in Somali is available in Andrzejewski, "Written Somali Literature;" B.W. Andrzejewski, "The Development of a National Orthography in Somalia and the Modernization of the Somali Language," *Horn of Africa* 1, no. 3 (1978): 39-45; B.W. Andrzejewski, "The Development of Somali as a National Medium of Education and Literature," *African Languages/Langues Africaines* 5, no. 2 (1979): 1-9; B.W. Andrzejewski, "Prose Fiction Writing in Somali, 1967-1981," *Proceedings of the Second International Congress of Somali Studies*, pp. 379-410; the introduction to M.J. Cawl, *Ignorance Is the Enemy of Love* (London: Zed Press, 1982), which is a novel, translated with introduction and notes by B.W. Andrzejewski; and in Gérard, *African Language Literatures*.

25. Serialized in *Xiddigta Oktoobar* 8: 81-85, 87-88 (1981), p. 3 [in each issue]. This passage is taken from issue 87.

Cassanelli: *Society and Culture in the Riverine Region of Southern Somalia*

1. In this essay, I use the term *riverine* to include both the areas along the two major rivers in Somalia and the large region located between them.

2. Massimo Colucci, *Principi di diritto consuetudinario della Somalia italiana meridionale* (Florence, 1924).

3. I.M. Lewis, "From Nomadism to Cultivation: The Expansion of Political Solidarity in Southern Somalia," in *Man in Africa*, ed. Mary Douglas and Phyllis Kaberry (London: Travistock, 1969).

4. Virginia Luling, "The Social Structure of Southern Somali Tribes" (Ph.D. diss., University of London, 1971).

5. Ibid., pp. 49-51; and Michele Pirone, *Sguardo alla societa somala e ai suoi problemi in generale: vol. 3. Appunti di sociologia generale* (Mogadishu, 1965).

6. Colucci, *Somalia italiana*, pp. 109-10, 114; Lewis, "Nomadism to Cultivation," p. 69.

7. Bernd Heine, "The Sam Languages: A History of Rendille, Boni, and Somali," *Afriasiatic Linguistics* 6, no. 2 (1978): 1-93; Christopher Ehret and Mohamed Nuuh Ali, "Soomaali Classification," *Proceedings of the Second International Congress of Somali Studies, University of Hamburg August 1-6, 1983*, ed. Thomas Labahn (Hamburg: Helmut Buske Verlag, 1984): 201-269.

8. Muusa H.I. Galaal, "Stars, Seasons, and Weather in Somali Pastoral Traditions" (unpublished manuscript, 1970).

9. Steven A. Brandt, George A. Brook, and Thomas H. Gresham, "Quaternary Paleoenvironments and Prehistoric Human Occupation of Northern Somalia," *Proceedings of the Second International Congress of Somali Studies*, pp. 7-21.

10. Nello Puccioni, "Antropologia e etnografia delle genti della Somalia," *Etnografia e paletnologia* (Bologna, 1936), vol. 3, pp. 82-87.

11. Enrico Cerulli, *Scritti vari editi ed inediti* (Rome: Amministrazione Fiduciaria Italiana della Somalia, 1957, 1959), vol. 1, pp. 54-57, vol. 2, pp. 115-21. Vinigi L. Grottanelli, "The Peopling of the Horn of Africa," in *East Africa and the Orient: Cultural Synthesis in Pre-colonial Times*, ed. Neville Chittick and Robert I. Rotberg (New York: 1975), pp. 61-68.

12. B.W. Andrzejewski, "The Position of Linguistic Minorities in Somalia" (unpublished manuscript, 1970).

13. Lee V. Cassanelli, "Social Constructs on the Somali Frontier: Bantu Ex-slave Communities in Nineteenth Century Somaliland," in *The Internal African Frontier*, ed. Igor Kopytoff (Bloomington: Indiana University Press, forthcoming).

14. Cerulli, *Scritti vari*, vol. 1, pp. 57ff; I.M. Lewis, "The Somali Conquest of the Horn of Africa," *Journal of African History* 1 (1960): 213-30; Herbert S. Lewis, "The Origins of the Galla and Somali," *Journal of African History* 7 (1966): 27-46; Heine, "Sam Languages."

15. Lee. V. Cassanelli, *The Shaping of Somali Society: Reconstructing the History of a Pastoral People, 1600-1900* (Philadelphia: University of Pennsylvania Press, 1982), pp. 84-118.

16. Ibid.

17. Luling, "Social Structure," pp. 69-70.

18. Galaal, "Stars, Seasons, and Weather," p. 66.

Grottanelli: *Somali Wood Engravings*

1. Enrico Cerulli, *Scritti vari editi ed inediti* (Rome: Amministrazione Fiduciaria Italiana della Somalia, 1957), vol. 1, pp. 135-37, 166.

2. J.S. Kirkman, "Azanici Centri," *Enciclopedia Universale dell'Arte* (Venice and Rome, 1958), vol. 2, pp. 285-92.

3. C.H. Stigand, *The Land of Zinj* (London: 1913), frontispiece plate.

4. H. Sassoon, *Guide to the Ruins of Kunduchi* (Dar-es-Salaam, 1966), pp. 4, 21.

5. A. Grohmann, "Arabi pre-islamici centri e tradizioni," *Enciclopedia Universale dell'Arte* (Venice and Rome, 1958), vol. 1, pp. 499-523.

6. Enrico Cerulli, "Cuscitiche Culture," *Enciclopedia Universale dell'Arte* (Venice and Rome, 1958), vol. 4, pp. 175-81, pl. 97.

7. Nello Puccioni, "Antropologia e etnografia delle genti della Somalia," *Etnografia e paletnologia* (Bologna, 1936), vol. 3, pp. 52-53.

8. Illustrations in Bottego, *Il Guiba esplorato* (1896), p. 398.

9. F. Stuhlmann, *Handwerk und Industrie in Ostafrika* (Hamburg, 1910), p. 111.

10. Cf. illustrations of similar types in Baudi di Vesme and Candeo, "Un' escursione nel Paradiso dei Somali," *Bollettino della Società Geografica Italiana*, ser. 3, vol. 4 (Rome, 1893), p. 194; and G. Révoil, *Dix mois à la côte orientale d'Afrique: La vallée du Darror et le Cap Guardafui* (Paris, 1888), p. 341, figs. 4 and 6.

11. F. Stuhlmann, *Handwerk und Industrie*, fig. 62. Cf. variations of the same type in U. Ferrandi, *Lugh, emporio commercial sul Guiba* (Rome, 1903), p. 219, and the elaborately engraved types used by the northernmost Cushitic group of tribes, the Beja (Buhler and Hinderling, "Beduin aus Nordostafrika," [Basel: Museum für Völkerkunde Basel, Sonderausstellung, 12 April-30 September, 1957], p. 25).

12. *Sagaf* in Baudi di Vesme and Candeo, "Un'escursione," p. 194; *sakafa* in Ferrand, *Les çomalis* (Paris, 1903), p. 202; *sakaf* in unpublished museum archive documents.

13. Ferrandi, *Lugh*, p. 220; Stuhlmann, *Handwerk und Industrie*, p. 111.

14. A. Mochi, "Gli oggetti etnografici delle popolazioni etiopiche posseduti dal Museo Nazionale di Antropologia in Firenze," *Archivio per l'Antropologia e la Etnologia* 30 (Florence, 1900), p. 151 (author's translation). I have followed up, and regrettably found untenable, the opinion of this author, according to which the ornamental patterns engraved on Somali spoons are reminiscent of geometrical motifs incised on Upper Egyptian prehistorical or protohistorical pottery described in Schweinfurth, "Ornamentik der ältern Kultur-Epoche Ägyptens," *Zeitschrift für Ethnologia* 29 (1897): 394.

15. The finest specimens known to me possibly produced by a single artisan were collected in 1892 by G. Candeo in the Upper Webi area. Specimens from Mahaddei Wen area in Pogliani collection, acquired by the museum in 1883. It should be noted that there is no apparent style difference between objects collected in the north, center, or south of Somalia.

16. J. Borelli, *Ethiopia méridionale* (Paris, 1890), p. 490. The collection of L. Robecchi-Bricchetti, acquired by the museum in 1889, includes two engraved spoons from the Harar Galla, similar in shape and design to Somali specimens, but of coarser execution. Cf. the six drawings of corresponding Somali implements illustrated in this traveler's book *(Somalia e Benadir,* Milano, 1899, p. 343). Haberland *(Galla Süd-Ätiopiens,* Stuttgart, 1963), who visited and studied the southern Galla in recent years, gives the illustration of a fine comb and spoon of Somali workmanship and says that these "pretty patterns and incised plaits" are not common among the Galla (p. 267).

17. E.F. Rohrer, *Beiträge zur Kenntnis der materiellen Kultur der Amhara* (Schönburg and Bern, 1932), pl. 6.

18. W.W. Battiss, G.H. Franz, J.W. Frossert, and H.P. Junod, *The Art of Africa* (Pietermaritzburg, 1958), p. 126.

19. F. von Laschan, "Beiträge zur Völkerkunde," *Erste deutsche Kolonial-Ausstellung* (Berlin, 1897), pl. 45; and V.L. Grottanelli, "Asiatic Influences on Somali Culture," *Ethnos* 12 (1947): 153-81.

20. E. Torday and T.A. Joyce, "Notes ethnographiques sur les peuples communément appelés Bakuba, ainsi que sur les peuplades apparentées, les Bushongo," *Annales du Musée du Congo Belge* (Brussels, 1911), pp. 215-18.

21. P. Paulitschke, *Ethnographie Nordafrikas* (Berlin, 1893-1896), vol. 2, pp. 160-63.

22. Cf. Cerulli, *Scritti vari,* passim.

23. P. Paulitschke, *Beiträge zur Ethnographie und Anthropologie der Somâl, Galla und Harari* (Leipzig, 1888), p. 39 (author's translation), and Paulitschke, *Ethnographie Nordafrikas,* vol. 1, pp. 235-36.

24. Stuhlmann, *Handwerk und Industrie,* pp. 111-12 (author's translation).

25. Puccioni, "Antropologia e etnografia," p. 31.

26. I.M. Lewis, "Peoples of the Horn of Africa," *Ethnographic Survey of Africa, North East Africa* (London: International African Institute, 1955), p. 83.

27. Apart from the Museo Pigorini, collections of these art objects exist in the Museo Africano, Rome, in the Museo Antropologia, Florence, and in the Museo della Garesa, Mogadiscio. The collections of Fort Jesus Museum, Mombasa, are of obvious importance for any further comparative research.

Note: Grateful acknowledgments are due to the Museo Nazionale Preistorico-Etnografico, Luigi Pigorini, Rome, for allowing publication of the reproductions [in the original publication of this article]. The author expresses his thanks to Dr. Valeria Petrucci of the museum staff for her collaboration in sorting out the objects and consulting archive documents concerning them. [Editor's note: "Somali Wood Engravings" first appeared in *African Arts* 1, no. 3 (1968): 8-16. It has been slightly edited for republication here.]

Lewis: *Islam in Somalia*

1. I.M. Lewis, *A Pastoral Democracy: A Study of Pastoralism and Politics among the Northern Somali of the Horn of Africa,* 2d ed. (New York: Africana, 1982).

2. I.M. Lewis, "From Nomadism to Cultivation: The Expansion of Political Solidarity in Southern Somalia," in *Man in Africa,* ed. Mary Douglas and Phyllis Kaberry (London: Travistock, 1969).

3. I.M. Lewis, "Conformity and Contrast in Somali Islam," in *Islam in Tropical Africa,* 2d. ed., ed. I.M. Lewis (London and Bloomington: International African Institute in association with Indiana University Press, 1980), pp. 240-52.

4. I.M. Lewis, "Sharif Yusuf Barkhadle: The Blessed Saint of Somali-land," *Proceedings of the Third International Conference of Ethiopian Studies* (Addis Ababa, 1969), pp. 75-82.

5. B.W. Andrzejewski and I.M. Lewis, *Somali Poetry: An Introduction* (Oxford: Clarendon Press, 1964); John William Johnson, *Heellooy Heelleellooy: The Development of the Genre Heello in Modern Somali Poetry* (Bloomington, Ind.: Research Center for the Language Sciences, 1974).

6. I.M. Lewis, *A Modern History of Somalia: Nation and State in the Horn of Africa,* 2d ed. rev. (London: Longman, 1980), pp. 18-39.

7. Ibid., pp. 63-91.

8. Said Sheikh Samatar, *Oral Poetry and Somali Nationalism: The Case of Sayyid Maḥammad 'Abdille Ḥassan* (Cambridge: Cambridge University Press, 1982). See also Yaasiin I. Keenadiid, *Ina Cabdille Xasan e la sua attivita letteraria* (Naples, 1984); and Aw Jaamac Cumar Ciise, *Taariikhdii Daraawiishta iyo Sayid Maxamad Cabdulle Xasan (1895-1921)* (Mogadishu: Akadeemiyaha Dhaqanka, 1976).

9. B.W. Andrzejewski, "The Rise of Written Somali Literature," *African Research and Documentation* 8/9 (1975): 7-14; David Laitin, *Politics, Language, and Thought: The Somali Experience* (Chicago: University of Chicago Press, 1977); Hussein Mohamed Adam, "Language, National Self-consciousness, and Identity—the Somali Experience," in *Nationalism and Self-determination in the Horn of Africa,* ed. I.M. Lewis (London: Ithica Press, 1983): 31-42.

10. I.M. Lewis, *Religion in Context: Cults and Charisma* (New York: Cambridge University Press, 1985), chap. 6.

CREDITS

Design Consultant: Pauline diBlasi
Catalogue Design: Kay Cole and Katheryne S. Loughran

Caption Editor: Mary Jo Arnoldi
Captions and Documentation: Kristyne S. Loughran

Bibliography: John W. Johnson

Photography

ALI ABDI ADAUE
145

CRISANNE ALBERS
119

LEE CASSANELLI
48, 54

PHOEBE FERGUSON
48, 50, 60, 63, 65, 77, 89, 92, 93, 108, 114, 116, 123, 126, 127, 131, 133, 134, 136, 137, 145, 154

DELMAR LIPP
49, 51, 52, 54, 55, 56, 57, 59, 61, 62, 65, 80, 83, 84, 85, 86, 90, 91, 115, 116, 117, 118, 120, 121, 122, 124, 128, 129, 130, 146, 148, 149, 150, 151, 152, 153, 155, 156, 157, 158, 159, 161, 162, 163, 164, 165, 166, 167

VIRGINIA LULING
68, 76, 78, 79, 80, 81

PHOTOGRAPHIC OFFICER, USS VREELAND
91

SAID SHEIKH SAMATAR
144

ABBY THOMAS
46, 47

MANFRED WEHRMANN
53, 58, 64, 82, 87, 88, 94, 95, 109, 110, 111, 130, 132, 135, 147

Cover: Carved door on a coral stone house in Xamar Weyn (detail). Photograph Manfred Wehrmann, Design Kay Cole

Printed and Bound in the USA by W.M. Brown & Son, Inc., Richmond, Virginia

Illustrations Virginia Corona and Salvatore Strazza
97, 98, 99, 100, 101, 102
Objects property of Museo L. Pigorini, Rome.

SELECTED BIBLIOGRAPHY

For the reader who wishes to learn more about Somalia and its people, we suggest the following books. While this list is by no means exhaustive, the works included here provide a broad perspective on Somalia. Most of these books have extensive bibliographies, which can serve as a further guide to the literature for the more ambitious reader.

Andrzejewski, B.W., and I.M. Lewis. *Somali Poetry: An Introduction.* Oxford: Clarendon Press, 1964.

Bhardwaj, Raman G. *The Dilemma of the Horn of Africa.* New Delhi: Sterling Pub., 1979.

Cassanelli, Lee V. *The Shaping of Somali Society: Reconstructing the History of a Pastoral People, 1600-1900.* Philadelphia: University of Pennsylvania Press, 1982.

Castagno, Margaret. *Historical Dictionary of Somalia.* Metuchen, N.J.: Scarecrow Press, 1975.

Drysdale, John. *The Somali Dispute.* London: Pall Mall Press, 1964.

Hassan Sheikh Mumin. *Leopard among the Women: Shabeelnaagood: A Somali Play.* Translated and with introduction by B.W. Andrzejewski. London: Oxford University Press, 1974.

Hess, Robert L. *Italian Colonialism in Somalia.* Chicago: University of Chicago Press, 1966.

Johnson, John William. *Heellooy Heelleellooy: The Development of the Genre Heello in Modern Somali Poetry.* Bloomington, Ind.: Research Center for the Language Sciences, 1974.

Laitin, David. *Politics, Language, and Thought: The Somali Experience.* Chicago: University of Chicago Press, 1977.

Laurence, Margaret. *A Tree for Poverty: Somali Poetry and Prose.* Shannon: Irish University Press, 1970.

Lewis, I.M. *A Modern History of Somalia: Nation and State in the Horn of Africa.* 2d ed. rev. London: Longman, 1980.

————. *A Pastoral Democracy: A Study of Pastoralism and Politics among the Northern Somali of the Horn of Africa.* 2d ed. New York: Africana, 1982.

————, ed. *Nationalism and Self-determination in the Horn of Africa.* London: Ithaca Press, 1983.

Said Sheikh Samatar. *Oral Poetry and Somali Nationalism: The Case of Sayyid Moḥammad 'Abdille Hassan.* Cambridge: Cambridge University Press, 1982.

Touval, Saadia. *Somali Nationalism: International Politics and the Drive for Independence in the Horn of Africa.* Cambridge: Harvard University Press, 1963.